Hero or Villain?

Claims and Counterclaims

John Brown
Armed Abolitionist

Alison Morretta

Cavendish Square
New York

Published in 2019 by Cavendish Square Publishing, LLC
243 5th Avenue, Suite 136, New York, NY 10016

Copyright © 2019 by Cavendish Square Publishing, LLC

First Edition

No part of this publication may be reproduced, stored in a retrieval system, or transmitted in any form or by any means—electronic, mechanical, photocopying, recording, or otherwise—without the prior permission of the copyright owner. Request for permission should be addressed to Permissions, Cavendish Square Publishing, 243 5th Avenue, Suite 136, New York, NY 10016. Tel (877) 980-4450; fax (877) 980-4454.

Website: cavendishsq.com

This publication represents the opinions and views of the author based on his or her personal experience, knowledge, and research. The information in this book serves as a general guide only. The author and publisher have used their best efforts in preparing this book and disclaim liability rising directly or indirectly from the use and application of this book.

All websites were available and accurate when this book was sent to press.

Library of Congress Cataloging-in-Publication Data

Names: Morretta, Alison, author.
Title: John Brown : Armed Abolitionist / Alison Morretta.
Description: First edition. | New York, NY : Cavendish Square Publishing,
LLC, 2019. | Series: Hero or Villain?: Claims and Counterclaims | Includes bibliographical references and index. |
Audience: 7-12. Identifiers: LCCN 2017058828 (print) | LCCN 2017060358 (ebook) |
ISBN 9781502635211 (eBook) | ISBN 9781502635204 (library bound) |
ISBN 9781502635228 (pbk.) Subjects: LCSH: Brown, John, 1800-1859--Juvenile literature. |
Abolitionists--United States--Biography--Juvenile literature. | Harpers Ferry (W. Va.)--History--John Brown's Raid, 1859--Juvenile literature. | Slavery--United States--History--Juvenile literature. | Antislavery movements--United States--History--Juvenile literature.
Classification: LCC E451 (ebook) | LCC E451 .M87 2019 (print) | DDC 973.7/116092 [B] --dc23
LC record available at https://lccn.loc.gov/2017058828

Editorial Director: David McNamara
Editor: Michael Spitz
Copy Editor: Rebecca Rohan
Associate Art Director: Amy Greenan
Designer: Amy Greenan/Christina Shults
Production Coordinator: Karol Szymczuk
Photo Research: J8 Media

The photographs in this book are used by permission and through the courtesy of:
Cover, Hi-Story/Alamy Stock Photo; Chapter opener used throughout book, Anonymous Portuguese (1502)/Biblioteca Estense Universitaria, Modena, Italy/Wikimedia Commons/File: Cantino planisphere (1502).jpg/Public Domain; p. 4 Chronicle/Alamy Stock Photo; p. 7 Library of Congress/Corbis/VCG/Getty Images; p. 8 Unknown/From an old postcard, 1918/Wikimedia Commons/File: Adelbert College, Western Reserve University, Cleveland, Ohio.jpg/Public Domain; pp. 10, 23, 31, 60, 64 North Wind Picture Archives; p. 13 Liljenquist Family Collection of Civil War Photographs, Library of Congress Prints and Photographs Division; p. 15 Unknown/Wikimedia Commons/File: Map of Free and Slave States.jpg/Creative Commons CC0 1.0 Universal Public Domain Dedication (https://creativecommons.org/public domain/zero/1.0/deed.en); p. 18 John Hooff/Printed at the Alexandria Gazette Office, Alexandria, VA, 19 February 1851/Cowan's Auctions/Wikimedia Commons/File: Female Runaway Slave, Illustrated Reward Broadside, Alexandria, Virginia, 1851.jpg/Public Domain; p. 21 Published by J.T. Bowen, Library of Congress Prints and Photographs Division; p. 33 Internet Archive Book Images, 1911(https://www.flickr.com/people/126377022@N07)/Wikimedia Commons /File: Essentials of United States history (1911) (14593356100).jpg/Public Domain; p. 34 Mark Reinstein/Corbis Historical/Getty Images; p. 37 Black & Batcheller, Jan 21 1864, Boston Mass, Library of Congress Prints and Photographs Division p. 39 George Kendall Warren (1834–1884)/National Archives and Records Administration, NAID 558770/Wikimedia Commons/File: Frederick Douglass portrait.jpg/Public Domain; p. 41 Charles Phelps Cushing/ClassicStock/Alamy Stock Photo; p. 45 Unknown/Wikimedia Commons/File: State Historical Society of Missouri/Wikimedia Commons/File: Sacking-lawrence.jpg/Public Domain; p. 47 Photo Researchers/Science History Images/Alamy Stock Photo; p. 56 MPI/Archive Photos/Getty Images; p. 62 Corbis/Getty Images; p. 67 Wm. Pearl, own work/Wikimedia Commons/File: 'The Last Moments of John Brown' by Thomas Hovenden, De Young Museum.JPG/CC0 1.0 Universal Public Domain Dedication; p. 73 Unattributed, Somersworth/Virginia Governor (1856-1859) Executive Papers of Governor Henry A. Wise, 1856-1859, Accession 36710, State Government Records Collection, The Library of Virginia, Richmond, VA/Wikimedia Commons/File: John Brown - Treason broadside, 1859.png/Public Domain, p. 79 Edward Williams Clay/Library of Congress Prints and Photographs Division; p. 84 Courtesy, Ohio History Connection, AL03156.tif; p. 87 New York Public Library scan/Wikimedia Commons/File: Nat Turner & his confederates in conference (NYPL Hades-256680-EM15325).jpg/Public Domain; p. 88 GraphicaArtis/Archive Photos/Getty Images; p. 91 Unknown/West Virginia & Regional History Center, https://storercollege.lib.wvu.edu/catalog/wvulibraries:1263/Wikimedia Commons/File: Storer College Students with School Banner, Harpers Ferry, W. VA.tif/Public Domain; p. 93 AP Photo/The Journal Newspaper, Ron Agniir;
p. 95 Bob Daemmrich/AFP/Getty Images.

Printed in the United States of America

CONTENTS

Chapter One   5
The Road to Harpers Ferry

Chapter Two   15
John Brown's America

Chapter Three   37
Carrying the War into Africa

Chapter Four   63
Martyr or Murderer?

Chapter Five   91
His Soul Marches On

Glossary   100
Chronology   102
Further Information   104
Selected Bibliography   106
Index   110
About the Author   112

A portrait of John Brown, created around 1903

The Road to Harpers Ferry

Chapter One

John Brown's controversial approach to abolition would lead him to the battleground territory of Kansas and ultimately to the hangman's noose in Virginia. He was unique among abolitionists of his time: a white man who believed not only that slavery was evil, but that all people should be treated as equal. This extended to both African American and Native peoples. Most white abolitionists in the nineteenth century held racial prejudice even while fighting the institution of slavery, but it was not so with John Brown. This was a direct result of his childhood, which was spent on the frontier among people of different races. His strict religious upbringing also contributed to his view of the world and the moral evils he saw within it.

Early Life

John Brown was born in 1800, in Torrington, Connecticut, to Owen Brown and Ruth Mills Brown. The Brown family had revolution in its blood. Brown's early ancestors were New England Puritans, who may have traveled to colonial America on the *Mayflower*. His maternal and paternal grandfathers both fought in the Revolutionary War.

Owen Brown was a strict Calvinist who believed in abolition and racial equality. He passed these traits on to his son, who would take them much further in his life than Owen did. Brown's mother died in childbirth when he was just eight years old, and the loss hit him very hard. His father remarried soon after, but John was never close to his stepmother, Sally Root.

Owen Brown was a tanner (leather worker) and owned a small farm. John Brown would later take up his father's businesses before dedicating himself to abolition. Owen's businesses struggled in Connecticut. In 1805, the Brown family moved to the frontier community of Hudson, Ohio. Hudson is located in what was then known as Connecticut's Western Reserve (territory previously owned by the state of Connecticut in what is now northeast Ohio).

The Browns were among the first white settlers in Hudson, which was founded in 1799. When the first white settlers moved to the Western Reserve, the majority population was made up of Native peoples, who far outnumbered white settlers. Young John Brown, who was five years old when he moved to Hudson, grew up in a multicultural, multiracial society. Unlike some of their neighbors, the Browns were

The birthplace of John Brown, located in Torrington, Connecticut

Owen Brown was one of the founders of Ohio's Western Reserve College, which was associated with the abolitionist movement.

friendly with the Native peoples. They did not discriminate against their nonwhite neighbors on the basis of race or ethnicity, which is something that Brown would emulate in his adult life and teach to his own children. Owen was one of the founders of Western Reserve College (now Case Western Reserve University), which was associated with the early abolitionist movement.

Nineteenth-century westward expansion was fueled, in part, by the desire of white Protestant Christians to spread their faith across the entire country. This included "civilizing" the Native peoples by converting them to Christianity. The Browns were different. Although Owen and Ruth were both intensely devout Calvinists, they did not try to force their religion on anyone of different spiritual beliefs. They peacefully coexisted with the Native peoples and treated them as they would any other person.

Brown's First Experience with Slavery

John Brown's first experience with slavery occurred when he was very young. While John enjoyed reading (especially the Bible), he was not particularly interested in school and preferred working for his father, who welcomed the help. During the War of 1812, Owen was granted a government contract to deliver beef to the US Army stationed in Detroit. Owen allowed twelve-year old John to make the cattle drive alone. On the way, he stayed with a family who owned a slave child, a boy around John's age.

John saw the child being beaten and mistreated at the hands of the people who were treating John with kindness. In Brown's eyes, the boy was no different from him aside from the color of his skin, and he was horrified at the cruelty he witnessed. He would later write in a letter to Henry Stearns (son of abolitionist George Stearns, who would fund Brown's raid) that this experience "made him a most determined Abolitionist" and led him to declare "eternal war with Slavery." He reflected on "the wretched, hopeless condition, of Fatherless & Motherless slave children: for such children have neither Fathers nor Mothers to protect & provide for them." Having lost his own mother, Brown was particularly sensitive to the fact that slave children were sold away from their parents.

John Brown's Faith

Like his father, John Brown was an intensely religious man. He was of the traditional New England Puritan tradition called Calvinism. Calvinists believe in predestination and

It was common for children, like the slave child pictured in this illustration, to start laboring for their masters at a young age.

the absolute sovereignty of God—also known as Divine Providence—in which all things are predetermined by an omnipotent God. Calvinists also believe in the total depravity of man, which is the concept that everyone is inherently sinful and motivated by self-interest. In the Calvinist tradition, only God's grace can grant salvation. This is different from other Protestant traditions at the time whose adherents (including many abolitionists) believed that salvation could be achieved through good works.

For Calvinists, people were responsible for their actions on Earth and atoning for their sins, but earthly deeds had no direct correlation to whether one would be granted God's grace. One was either chosen or not, and one's fate was determined before humanity even existed. With this religious background, Brown believed that his actions on Earth were the will of God. Brown was influenced by the vengeful God of the Old Testament and considered himself one of God's warriors. Slavery was a moral evil and a sin against God's children, and Brown believed he was predestined to carry out God's vengeance for the sin of slavery by any means necessary. For Brown, that meant picking up a Bowie knife and a rifle and terrorizing anyone who supported the sin of slavery.

Organized Abolitionist Movement

John Brown was an abolitionist in his beliefs but did not participate in the organized movement that began in the early nineteenth century. The main abolitionist organization during Brown's time was the American Anti-Slavery Society (AASS). The AASS was established in Philadelphia in 1833. Its founders were William Lloyd Garrison, publisher of the abolitionist newspaper the *Liberator*, and New York businessmen Arthur and Lewis Tappan. The AASS called for the immediate emancipation of slaves without compensation and sought reform through moral suasion—effecting change through the moral purification of the people. They also rejected the Constitution as a proslavery document.

In 1840, some members (including the Tappans) broke away and formed the American and Foreign Anti-Slavery Society (AFASS). Members of the AFASS believed that the Garrisonian approach to abolition, which attacked the government and advocated rights

A portrait of prominent abolitionst William Lloyd Garrison

for women in addition to racial equality, was too radical to succeed. The AFASS believed that political reform was the only viable way to attack the institution of slavery. Despite these differences, the vast majority of mainstream abolitionists were against the use of violent tactics to fight slavery.

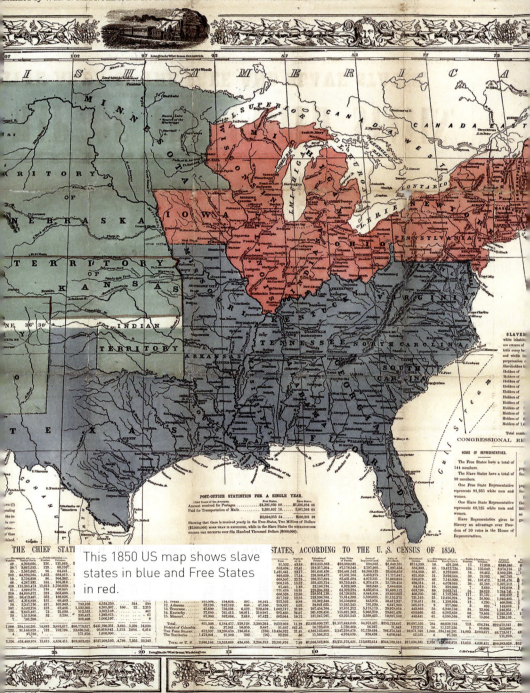

This 1850 US map shows slave states in blue and Free States in red.

John Brown's America

Chapter Two

John Brown lived during a time when America was rapidly changing and expanding. The nineteenth century was a time of sectional tension and conflict that ultimately led to war, but the stage was set for this conflict long before John Brown was born in 1800. The movement for the abolition of slavery reached its peak during the early- to mid-nineteenth century. As early as America's colonial period, there were individuals who objected to slavery in the New World. During the American Revolution, the democratic ideals of freedom and equality that the colonists fought for were incompatible with slavery. This contradiction is evident in two of the nation's most important founding documents, the Declaration of Independence and the United

States Constitution. The former called for equality and liberty, and the latter codified slavery into the very fabric of the United States of America.

Declaration of Independence

The preamble to the Declaration of Independence famously states: "We hold these truths to be self-evident, that all men are created equal, that they are endowed, by their Creator, with certain unalienable Rights, that among these are Life, Liberty, and the pursuit of Happiness." The Declaration was drafted by Thomas Jefferson of Virginia. Jefferson was one of many members of the Continental Congress, including George Washington, James Madison, and Benjamin Franklin among others, who owned slaves at the time this document was created—a document that declared liberty to be a fundamental American right. Many of the slaveholding delegates struggled morally with the institution of slavery. In the debates that surrounded the establishment of the Constitution, the question of slavery was political, not moral. Jefferson and many of his contemporaries believed that slavery would die out on its own, and they felt the more pressing issue was bringing the Southern states into the Union.

Slavery in the Constitution

The words "slave" and "slavery" were not used in the United States Constitution, but the document still managed to codify and strengthen the institution of slavery in the United

States. Article 1, Section 2 of the Constitution included what became known as the Three-Fifths Compromise. This clause states, in part, that representatives and taxation "shall be determined by adding to the whole Number of free Persons, including those bound to Service for a Term of Years, and excluding Indians not taxed, three fifths of all other Persons." The terms "other persons" is used in lieu of the word "slaves."

Another section that directly addressed slavery is Article 1, Section 9, which stated that Congress could not abolish the Atlantic slave trade or ban importation of slaves until 1808—twenty years after the Constitution went into effect. The most significant part of the Constitution with regard to slavery was Article 4, Section 2, Clause 3, known as the Fugitive Slave Clause. This stated, "No Person held to Service or Labour in one State, under the Laws thereof, escaping into another, shall, in Consequence of any Law or Regulation therein, be discharged from such Service or Labour, but shall be delivered up on Claim of the Party to whom such Service or Labour may be due." This clause gave slaveholders a constitutional right to reclaim their property. Without it, many Southern states may not have ratified the Constitution.

Without once using the word "slave," the Constitution established slavery as law and solidified the rights of slaveholders to recapture their slaves anywhere in the nation, including locations where slavery had been or would be abolished. The compromises regarding slavery that were included in the final version of the United States Constitution were not a permanent solution to the problem.

20 DOLLARS REWARD!

☞ Ranaway in the month of June last, from the subscriber residing in Alexandria, Va., NEGRO WOMAN, LUCY, called

LUCY PAYNE,

Aged about 50 years, well set and fleshy; full breast, front teeth decayed, greyish hair, the nail on one of her four-fingers injured, a small red mark on one of her cheeks, about 5 feet 2 or 3 inches high, wears a handkerchief generally on her head. I will give the above reward if delivered to me, or $10 if secured in jail.

It is believed that she is harbored in, or near Washington or Tennelly Town; she has a husband residing in Washington City, called George Payne.   JOHN HOOFF.

Alexandria, Va., February 19, 1851.

[PRINTED AT THE ALEXANDRIA GAZETTE OFFICE.]

This 1851 broadside advertises a reward of twenty dollars for the return of a runaway slave. After 1850, Northerners faced severe penalties if they did not help capture fugitives.

With their rights to slave property constitutionally granted, the slave system in the South became more firmly entrenched in that region. As the United States expanded westward in the nineteenth century, the compromises that had kept a balance of power between the North and the South started to break down.

Westward Expansion

The late eighteenth and early nineteenth centuries were a time of great change in the United States. There was massive population growth as well as an influx of European immigrants. The Industrial Revolution was transforming the economy from a farm-based to a market-based system. As the country expanded to meet its needs, the question of whether or not slavery would be allowed in newly acquired land was a constant source of debate.

It was not just the question of slavery driving the settlement of the American West. At the time, the policy of imperialistic expansion known as manifest destiny was prevalent. The concept of manifest destiny is that white American Christians have a God-given duty to settle the whole continent, spreading the American ideals of democracy and liberty and bringing "civilization" to the indigenous peoples of the West. The desire to spread American (i.e., white Christian) values westward to the Pacific was a driving force during this period and led to increased tensions between the North and South.

In 1803, the single largest land acquisition in American history, the Louisiana Purchase, took place under President Thomas Jefferson. Jefferson was an early supporter of westward expansion. He believed that the ideal America was a rural, agrarian society and that the individual landholding farmer best represented the American values of liberty and equality. At this time, America's economy was still based on agriculture, so it was important to acquire new land to cultivate. The Louisiana Purchase doubled the size of the United States and gave Americans full access to the Mississippi River and the Port of New Orleans, which were both important trade routes. The new territory stretched west from the Mississippi River to the Rocky Mountains, and from the Gulf of Mexico in the South to Canada in the North.

The Missouri Compromise

When proslavery Missouri applied for statehood in 1819, there was an equal amount of slave states and Free States (eleven each). If accepted into the Union, Missouri would throw the balance in favor of the slave states. Missouri's statehood was fiercely debated in Congress, and an agreement called the Missouri Compromise was reached in 1820. The Compromise was an agreement between proslavery and antislavery factions in Congress to regulate slavery in the west. It prohibited slavery in all Louisiana Purchase territory north of the 36°30′ latitude line (except Missouri itself). Maine was admitted as a Free State to maintain balance in the Union. This was a short-term fix for the problem, but it held for the next thirty years.

Anti-Abolitionist Violence in the North

The aggressive response was not limited to the South. Many prejudiced white Northerners were opposed to the idea of racial equality and the growing population of black people in

This illustration depicts the May 17, 1838, burning of Pennsylvania Hall in Philadelphia. A mob burned the building because it was constructed as a space for abolitionist meetings.

the Free States. The economy was also a contributing factor to proslavery sentiment. Northern textile manufacturing required Southern cotton, and there were many people who wanted slavery to continue so that the Northern economy would not be disrupted. Even in the Free States, abolitionists were subject to harassment, violence, and even murder.

The proslavery press often published reports of the abolitionists' activity and printed handbills urging people to take violent action against them. This was just adding fuel to the fire already burning in the North, especially in the abolitionist stronghold of Boston. There were already violent riots and lootings going on in Boston, which had a relatively large black population. When Garrison spoke out against this violence, a proslavery mob put a gallows (a structure used to hang criminals) in front of his home as a symbolic threat of lynching. In 1835, Garrison was captured and dragged through the streets, and he was forced to spend the night in jail for his own safety.

This extreme racial prejudice in a free city of the North was disturbing to the abolitionists, but attacks on freedom of speech and freedom of assembly were common responses by proslavery Northerners outraged by the abolitionists' ideas of disunion and racial equality.

The Murder of Elijah P. Lovejoy

The first martyr to the cause of abolition was newspaper editor Elijah P. Lovejoy. In July 1836, Lovejoy was driven out of Saint Louis, Missouri by a proslavery mob. The attacks on slavery and support of gradual emancipation Lovejoy published in his paper, the *St. Louis Observer*, angered many people in the slave state of Missouri. The mob destroyed his press, and he relocated to Alton, Illinois.

Lovejoy started a new abolitionist paper, the *Alton Observer*. Alton was a border town on the Mississippi River across from Saint Louis. Even though Illinois was a Free State, it was filled with supporters of slavery, including slave-catchers who made a living capturing fugitives coming across the river. Alton also had an active abolitionist community, with stops on the Underground Railroad, and the tension between the two factions often erupted in violence. Lovejoy's printing press was destroyed three times, and his home was attacked. On November 7, 1837, a mob set fire to the warehouse where his fourth press was, and Lovejoy was shot and killed while trying to stop them. The murder of a white abolitionist in a Free State caused many Northerners to join the abolitionist cause.

Texas and the Mexican-American War

The Republic of Texas won its independence from Mexico in 1836, and the debate over the annexation of Texas led to sectional tension. Texas legalized slavery and banned free black settlers, which made it hard for the US government to annex the republic. Texas, which was south of the Missouri Compromise line, was large enough to be divided into several territories that would enter the Union as slave states. This would cause a shift in the balance of power favoring the

This illustration depicts a proslavery mob burning the printing press of abolitionist Elijah P. Lovejoy in Alton, Illinois. Lovejoy was shot and killed and became a martyr to the abolitionists.

proslavery side. Because of its potential threat to the Union, Texas's annexation stalled in Congress for almost a decade.

A believer in the concept of manifest destiny, President James K. Polk pursued the annexation of Texas, and it was admitted as a slave state in 1845. When Texas entered the Union, there was a dispute with Mexico over the border. The United States claimed that Texas extended as far south as the Rio Grande River, while Mexico claimed that the border was further north. President Polk, who was in favor of the expansion of slavery, wanted to purchase land from Mexico and settle the dispute, but his offer was rejected. Fighting broke out when the United States sent troops to the border region, and the United States declared war on Mexico on May 13, 1846.

Not long after the Mexican-American War began, Congress began to debate the terms for negotiating the end of the conflict with Mexico. In August 1846, Pennsylvania Democrat David Wilmot introduced a brief addition to the war appropriations bill that was under consideration. Wilmot's proposal would prohibit slavery in any territory acquired from Mexico. It was highly offensive to Southerners, even though it was aimed more at protecting white settlers from having to compete with slave labor. Southerners also opposed it because it would create an overwhelming majority of Free States in Congress and deny them equal political representation. Although it did not pass the Senate, the Wilmot Proviso added to the growing hostility between the North and the South and raised the question of whether Congress had the power to regulate slavery.

The Treaty of Guadalupe Hidalgo officially ended the Mexican-American War on February 2, 1848. The United States agreed to pay Mexico $15 million (equal to over $437 million today) in exchange for more than 500,000 square miles (1,294,994 square kilometers) of new territory. This land, called the Mexican Cession, included the present-day states of California, Nevada, Utah, and New Mexico, as well as parts of Arizona, Colorado, Kansas, and Wyoming. This was the largest land acquisition to date and caused a series of Senate debates over the question of slavery in the territories.

The Compromise of 1850

During the 1840s, the United States expanded west to the Pacific, and new areas were opened to settlers. In 1850, after years of sectional conflict in Congress, an agreement was reached as to how to handle the new territory. The Compromise of 1850 was a bill drafted by Kentucky senator Henry Clay and Illinois senator Stephen A. Douglas that sought to restore harmony to the Union on the question of slavery in the Mexican Cession.

Henry Clay was a well-respected Kentucky senator who was known for his ability to broker deals in Congress (like the 1820 Missouri Compromise) that eased tension between the North and South. Clay was committed to maintaining the Union and believed that both sides needed to make concessions in order to keep the peace. On January 29, 1850, he proposed a number of resolutions in the Senate meant to solve the problems facing the nation after the US acquired the Mexican Cession.

California had applied for statehood as a Free State, and as a result, Congress delayed the admission of the state to the Union. Admitting California as free would throw off the balance between slave states and Free States and weaken the power of proslavery politicians. Clay knew that to gain a majority vote for the admission of California, concessions would need to be made to the South. Clay proposed the following: (1) California would be admitted as a Free State; (2) there would be no restriction by Congress on slavery in the territory acquired from Mexico; (3) Texas would give up the disputed land in exchange for $10 million to pay debts owed to Mexico; (4) the slave trade, but not slavery, would be abolished in Washington, DC; and (5) the Fugitive Slave Act would be tightened and more strictly enforced.

Clay's compromise left the slavery question in the territories open-ended. It neither prohibited or allowed slavery in the region. Clay proposed that Congress establish territorial governments without restrictions on slavery and allow the population to decide—a process called popular sovereignty. Clay's argument was that slavery was not likely to exist in the territories because the natural conditions of the land made it unsuitable, and therefore it was unnecessary for Congress to decide it. He also gave the example of California, where the people had chosen to enter the Union as a Free State.

Many Southern and Northern politicians reacted strongly against Clay's proposal because the extremists on each side felt they would be giving up too much. The proslavery South believed that accepting California as free while not gaining any slave territory from Mexico would create a huge imbalance of power in Congress. The Northern extremists believed that the stricter fugitive slave laws and the possible expansion of slavery into new territories were completely unacceptable.

The Fugitive Slave Act

No part of the Compromise of 1850 was more offensive to Northerners than the stricter Fugitive Slave Act. The new version of the 1793 law required citizens and officials in the Free States to assist in the capture of any black person claimed as a slave. The alleged fugitive had no right to a jury trial and could not testify, and the sworn testimony of a slave owner was considered enough evidence. Federal commissioners were appointed to handle these cases and were paid twice as much to return a fugitive than they were to set him or her free. Anyone who aided fugitives or helped them avoid capture was subject to a fine of $1,000 or six months' jail time.

This law endangered the free blacks of the North, who could more easily be kidnapped and sold into slavery. It forced antislavery Northerners to actively support the institution on free soil. Northerners saw it as an extension of slavery into the Free States by forcing individuals who were against slavery to violate their beliefs. It added fuel to the abolitionists' cause and increased participation in the Underground Railroad, a network of individuals who covertly helped fugitive slaves to avoid capture and escape to freedom in Canada.

The Kansas-Nebraska Act

What began as a bid for a northern route for the transcontinental railroad became one of the most controversial pieces of legislation passed in the years leading up to war. Senator Stephen Douglas of Illinois wanted the railroad to pass through the North, including the city of Chicago in his home state. He introduced a bill that would open up the Nebraska Territory to settlement with this goal in mind. The area that Douglas wanted to open to settlement was the unorganized territory that stretched from the Missouri River to the Rocky Mountains. This area contained fertile land. Under the Missouri Compromise, it would all be closed to slavery. The Compromise of 1850 left the status of the Missouri Compromise line uncertain since some of the Mexican Cession territory fell above the line established at 36°30' and part of the Free State of California was below it. Douglas's first proposal used popular sovereignty as a way to decide the slavery question but ignored the Missouri Compromise.

Proslavery Southerners rejected this initial plan and would not support the bill if it did not include a specific repeal of the Missouri Compromise line. Douglas knew he could never pass a bill to organize the territory without Southern support and that some concessions would need to be made. To appease the South, he revised the bill to include a repeal of the Missouri Compromise line and proposed dividing the territory in two, creating Nebraska in the North and Kansas in the South. The slavery question would be decided by popular sovereignty in both territories.

After months of debate in both the Senate and the House, the final version of the Kansas-Nebraska bill was signed into law by President Franklin Pierce on May 30, 1854. The Kansas-Nebraska Act created the territories of Kansas and Nebraska, which would "be received into the Union with or without slavery, as their constitution may prescribe at the time of admission." The act explicitly repealed the Missouri Compromise and included provisions for territorial governments and elections in which "the people [of Kansas and Nebraska were] perfectly free to form and regulate their domestic institutions in their own way."

Settling Kansas

After Kansas was opened up to white settlement, antislavery Northerners wanted to populate the region with people who would vote to prohibit slavery in the territory. Abolitionists and antislavery politicians organized societies and raised money to help move people from New England to Kansas. One of the most influential of these was the Massachusetts Emigrant Aid Company (later renamed the New England Emigrant Aid Company). The company lectured to recruit settlers from around New England and raised money to help with the cost of transporting people and establishing settlements.

The tension between proslavery and antislavery factions during the settlement of Kansas Territory often resulted in violence. The especially bloody period in the mid-1850s was dubbed "Bleeding Kansas."

The newly established Kansas Territory bordered the slave state of Missouri and became a battleground when Northern antislavery and Southern proslavery factions rushed to settle in the region. Because of rumors running through the South that thousands of armed Northerners were heading to the territory, armed border ruffians from Missouri crossed into Kansas to secure the territory for slavery. These men were urged by Missouri senator (and slave owner) David Atchison to enter the territory and vote illegally. Ruffians were armed with rifles and Bowie knives and engaged in intimidation tactics and fraud. They also voted, even though they were not residents. The number of ballots cast in the 1855 territorial election was much higher than the number of registered voters. The result was a proslavery government that enacted exceptionally harsh laws aimed at their opponents.

Under the proslavery Kansas territorial legislation, "An Act to Punish Offenses against Slave Property," it was decreed that only proslavery men were allowed to hold office and serve on juries. It became a felony offense to express antislavery views. Anyone caught helping fugitives would be sentenced to ten years in prison, and inciting or aiding a slave rebellion was punishable by death by hanging. In addition to these legislative restrictions, proslavery publications openly called for violence against antislavery settlers. John Stringfellow, in an 1855 editorial in the *Atchison Squatter Sovereign*, wrote, "We will continue to tar and feather, drown, lynch, and hang every white-livered abolitionist who dares to pollute our soil."

Free State settlers rejected the proslavery government they saw as illegitimate and formed a rival government later that year. The majority of these Free Staters were not abolitionists. They did not support the spread of slavery in the territory for purely economic reasons. Most Free Staters wanted Kansas to exclude black people—slave and free—from the territory. They did not want to compete with slave labor and, like many Northerners, they held extreme racial prejudice. To this end, the Topeka Constitution, adopted by Free State settlers in October 1855, included a "Negro Exclusion Clause." Even though many antislavery whites in Kansas wanted to exclude black settlers from the region, they were no different from radical abolitionists like John Brown in the eyes of the proslavery settlers. Anyone who did not support slavery in the territory was an enemy to the slave power, regardless of their views on race.

United States in 1821

A depiction of the slave states and Free State divide in the United States in 1821, one year after the Missouri Compromise.

As America grew larger, the question of whether new states would be admitted to the Union as slave or free dominated the national consciousness. In the years immediately preceding John Brown's raid on Harpers Ferry, the Kansas-Nebraska Territory was the focus of much of this debate, and the violent conflicts that erupted there were a preview of the bloody war to come.

Brown's original cabin at the John Brown Museum in Osawatomie, Kansas

Carrying the War into Africa

Chapter Three

John Brown and his family moved to Kansas in 1855, at a time when the region was embroiled in civil conflict over the question of slavery in the newly opened territory. It was in Kansas that John Brown fully committed to using terror tactics to fight slavery. It wasn't long before he found himself in Virginia, executing the raid he had been planning for over a decade. Harpers Ferry sealed Brown's fate, but Brown's willingness to use violent means to achieve justice for black Americans was evident long before any blood was shed.

The League of Gileadites

Brown responded swiftly to the Fugitive Slave Act of 1850. During the fall of that year, he turned his wool warehouse in Springfield, Massachusetts, into an Underground

Railroad station. In January 1851, he organized a black militia group that he named "The United States League of Gileadites." Brown believed in gender equality as well as racial equality, and the group was made up of forty-four black men and women, many of whom were fugitives. The organization's goal was to thwart slave-catchers and help fugitives escape to Canada.

Brown's instructions to the league are an early example of his willingness to use violence against the slave power. In his "Words of Advice to the United States League of Gileadites," Brown laid out a strategy in which the armed militia should attack a slave-catcher on sight and kill anyone who posed a threat to the militia members. They were then to retreat to nearby safe houses, owned by whites who were sympathetic to the cause. The homeowners would do their best to conceal the members of the league. If they were caught, their fellow Gileadites were instructed to go to the courtroom armed with gunpowder during the trial and then cause an explosion as a distraction so they could free the prisoner.

Brown's instructions included the following: "Do not delay one moment after you are ready: you will lose all your resolution if you do. Let the first blow be the signal for all to engage; and when engaged do not do your work by halves, but make clean work with your enemies." He also instructed members to "Stand by one another and by your friends, while a drop of blood remains; and be hanged, if you must, but tell no tales out of school. Make no confession." Even though he was actively breaking the law, Brown did not consider the league to be anti-American or treasonous. In fact, he

This portrait of abolitionist John Brown was published ten days after his execution and depicts the abolitionist at age fifty-nine, around the time of his attack on Harpers Ferry.

included the following in the "Agreement" section signed by league members: "As citizens of the United States of America, trusting in a just and merciful God, whose spirit and all-powerful aid we humbly implore, we will ever be true to the flag of our beloved country, always acting under it."

This agreement demonstrates Brown's belief that black people were American citizens—a view not shared by the United States government. Brown believed in an America in which all black people, slave or free, were equal citizens of the United States and deserving of the same rights and protections as whites. From this perspective, those who perpetuated the slave system were the treasonous ones, even if the nation's laws stated otherwise. To Brown, the current laws of the United States were a violation of divine law which included, among other things, the Golden Rule: treat others as you would want to be treated. Since Brown's religious faith was based in the absolute sovereignty of God, he had no patriotic obligation to follow laws made by sinful men who supported (or passively accepted) slavery. Brown's America was not the real America, and whether he liked it or not, he was subject to the laws of man.

Brown Meets Frederick Douglass

Frederick Douglass was the most influential black abolitionist of the nineteenth century and Brown greatly admired him. He first met Douglass in the winter of 1847–1848 in Springfield, Massachusetts. Brown shared with Douglass his early plans for the liberation of slaves, which he called the Subterranean Pass Way (SPW). He showed Douglass a

Abolitionist Frederick Douglass was a trusted friend and advisor to John Brown.

map of the Allegheny mountain range, which he planned to use as a base for a guerrilla operation to raid slave-owners' property and free slaves. Brown assumed that the fugitives would then join his army and participate in further raids. Brown's goal was twofold: to instill fear in the slaveholders by raiding their property and to bring national attention to slavery.

Organized slave rebellions, while rare in America, were a huge source of anxiety in the South—especially on plantations where blacks far outnumbered whites. A number of previous successful slave rebellions in Haiti and Jamaica were well known to Americans, as was the slave-led Nat Turner Rebellion in 1831. The slaveholders' fear of violent riots led to even harsher laws intended to keep slaves in line.

Slave states increased patrols, made it illegal to teach black people (slave or free) to read and write, and prohibited group gatherings, including religious congregations, without the presence of a white person.

Brown's plan was to draw on Southern anxiety and create an environment of fear and insecurity that would ultimately topple the slave system. Douglass did not believe that Brown's plan would succeed but came away from the meeting with great respect for Brown's commitment. In his abolitionist newspaper, the *North Star*, Douglass wrote of Brown that, "though a white gentleman, [he] is in sympathy a black man, and as deeply interested in our cause as though his own soul had been pierced with the iron of slavery."

The Osawatomie Browns

Brown urged his sons to move to Kansas and join the antislavery community there. In an August 21, 1854 letter he wrote to John Jr., Brown said that he supported any of his family who wanted to go Kansas "to help defeat Satan and his legions." Five of his sons—John Jr., Jason, Owen, Frederick, and Salmon—took the suggestion and settled near Osawatomie. Brown did not join them right away because he had promised his black neighbors in North Elba that he would help them establish their farming community. Meanwhile, armed proslavery men were flooding into Kansas Territory.

In May 1855, John Jr. wrote to his father about the situation in Kansas: "Every slaveholding state is furnishing men and money to fasten slavery upon this glorious land, by means no matter how foul." John Jr. told his father that they were ready and willing to fight but needed weapons to match the strength of their opponents. Meanwhile, the Browns—especially John Jr.—were making a name for themselves in the territory. Not long after their arrival in Kansas, a group of armed border ruffians approached them and asked about their political stance. John Jr. openly exclaimed, "We are Free State, and more than that, we are Abolitionists." Openly flouting the laws against antislavery sentiments put the Browns in danger of arrest or worse, but John Jr. did not hesitate to express his views.

John Brown heeded his sons' call, and in the months before he moved to Kansas, he attempted to raise funds and procure weapons. In June, Brown spoke at an abolitionist convention in Syracuse, New York, where he read John Jr.'s

This log cabin in Osawatomie, Kansas, was home to John Brown and his family in the mid-1850s.

letter and solicited donations for the crisis in Kansas. He picked up additional funds and guns in Ohio and arrived in Osawatomie in October 1855, settling at the family compound they had named Brown's Station.

The Wakarusa War

John Brown secured guns and ammunition to bring to Kansas, and the Browns were ready and willing to use them to defend themselves. The fear of retribution—both legal and violent—was very real for the Free State settlers in Kansas Territory, and the Browns were willing to meet this violence with violence. Armed conflict was already raging in the territory, and it was only getting worse. There were several incidents of violence against antislavery settlers, some of which resulted in murders that were never prosecuted. The Browns, already notorious for their abolitionist stance, were justifiably concerned that they would be targeted.

One incident, which occurred on November 21, 1855, led to the Wakarusa War—the first armed conflict in which John Brown was a participant. Proslavery settler Franklin Coleman shot Free Stater Charles Dow in the back as a result of a dispute over land rights. In the aftermath, proslavery sheriff Samuel J. Jones falsely arrested Dow's housemate, Jacob Branson. Branson was rescued by a posse of armed Free State men and taken to safety in Lawrence. As a result, Sheriff Jones went to Kansas governor Wilson Shannon to request that an armed militia be sent to Lawrence.

Jones led the militia, which was over one thousand men strong and made up of mostly drunken Missouri border ruffians, who gathered at the Wakarusa River near Lawrence. Free Staters, including John Brown and some of his sons, responded by arming themselves and heading to Lawrence to defend the town. By the time the Browns arrived at the Free State Hotel in Lawrence on December 7, they received news that an unarmed Free State man, Thomas Barber, had been killed by a group of Missourians. Free State leaders James Lane and Charles Robinson were negotiating with Governor Shannon to end the conflict, but Brown and others were planning an attack on the militia. Brown was made captain of the First Brigade of Kansas Volunteers and given command of a company of men called the Liberty Guard.

Although they were armed and ready, Brown and his men did not end up battling the proslavery forces. Lane and Robinson were able to convince Governor Shannon to call off the militia. Conflict was averted, but the truce did not last long. Brown came away from the Wakarusa incident convinced that the antislavery faction had gained ground and the territory would soon be a Free State. The battle for Kansas had only just begun. The Browns' reputation for militancy had only grown after Wakarusa, despite the fact that they did not fire a single shot.

The Sack of Lawrence

On April 23, 1856, Sheriff Jones was shot while trying to arrest some Free Staters. Jones survived but was driven out of Lawrence. In response, Judge Samuel Lecompte charged several Free State leaders with treason. On May 11, federal marshal J. B. Donaldson called for an attack on the town.

Hundreds of militiamen from Missouri and other Southern states heeded the call. On day of the attack, former Missouri senator David Rice Atchison gave a speech encouraging proslavery forces to use violence against the people of Lawrence. Atchison told them to "draw your revolvers and Bowie knives, and cool them in the heart's blood" of the "Hellish lying free-soilers" that populated the town. He instructed the men gathered to "burn, sack and destroy until every vestige of these Northern Abolitionists is wiped out. Never slacken or stop until every spark of Free State, free speech, free [blacks], or free in any shape, is quenched out of Kansas."

On May 21, 1856, the proslavery militia raided Lawrence, burning buildings, looting homes, and destroying antislavery printing presses. When Brown heard the news, he and his sons took up arms along with other members of the Pottawatomie Rifles, but by the time they got to Lawrence, it was already over. Brown was furious that the Free Staters did not put up a fight and decided that retaliation was necessary.

The Caning of Charles Sumner

On May 19–20, 1856, abolitionist senator Charles Sumner gave a speech, "The Crime Against Kansas," in response to the conflict in the territory. Sumner blamed the South for the violence caused by their "depraved longing for a new slave State … in the hope of adding to the power of slavery in the National Government." Sumner personally attacked South Carolina senator Andrew Butler. He stated that Butler "has chosen a mistress to whom he has made his vows … the harlot, Slavery." Sumner accused both Butler and Stephen

This illustration depicts the ruins of the Free State Hotel in Lawrence, Kansas, after the city was sacked by proslavery forces in 1856.

Douglas of "betray[ing] all the cherished sentiments of the fathers and the spirit of the Constitution, in order to give new spread to Slavery."

A few days after this speech, Butler's nephew, Congressman Preston Brooks, beat Sumner with his cane and knocked him unconscious on the floor of the senate. To Brooks, it was a matter of defending his family's honor—a very Southern concept. To Northerners, it was an act of antiabolitionist violence. It took three years for Sumner to fully recover and return to work, and he became a martyr to the Northern abolitionists. Likewise, Preston Brooks became a hero to the South.

John Brown and his men received word of the incident shortly before they set out for Pottawatomie Creek and were enraged by what they heard. Jason Brown, recalling his father's response to the news, said that, "At that blow the men went crazy … it seemed to be the finishing, decisive touch." He also claimed that his father, when advised to be cautious, stated, "I am eternally tired of hearing that word caution. It is nothing but the word of cowardice." The Sumner caning was the last straw for Brown, who had long been determined to take violent action against proslavery forces in Kansas and beyond.

The Pottawatomie Massacre

The massacre of proslavery men for which Brown became notorious was a response to general proslavery violence—most recently the Sack of Lawrence and the Sumner caning—but it had earlier roots in events that occurred in late April 1856. Judge Sterling G. Cato had issued arrest warrants for Brown and his sons on the grounds that they were known abolitionists. The court session was held in a tavern owned by Henry Sherman (known as "Dutch Henry"). Cato did not end up making any arrests despite the fact that several of the Browns gathered outside the tavern and loudly proclaimed the establishment of a militia—the Pottawatomie Rifles—pledged to resist the laws of the proslavery government. Present in the court that day were several men who would be slaughtered at Pottawatomie a month later: James P. Doyle (a member of the jury), his son William Doyle (a bailiff), and Allen Wilkinson (an attorney).

On the night of May 24, Brown set out for Pottawatomie Creek with a small group: his sons Frederick, Salmon, Oliver, and Owen; his son-in-law Henry Thompson; and two other

This mural, titled *Tragic Prelude*, was painted by John Steuart Curry in the late 1930s and depicts John Brown in battle during the "Bleeding Kansas" years.

associates, James Townsley and Theodore Weiner. In what became known as the "Pottawatomie Massacre," Brown's group dragged five men from their homes and brutally murdered them in front of their families. While all the victims were supporters of Kansas's proslavery side, none of them actually owned slaves. Brown's victims were all men either directly involved in the April trial or related to men who were involved: James Doyle and his sons William and Drury, Allen Wilkinson, and William Sherman. William was the brother of "Dutch Henry," who was not at home when the attack occurred or he would have been killed as well.

Carrying the War into Africa

Brown's men attacked their victims viciously, hacking them to death with broadswords and leaving them to bleed out. There is some question as to John Brown's level of involvement in the actual killings. He claimed that he only directed the action but did not kill anyone himself. He did shoot James Doyle in the head, but he always maintained that Doyle was already dead when he shot him. After the murders, Brown and his men stole horses and returned to their camp on Middle Ottawa Creek, where they met up with the other Pottawatomie Rifles, including John Jr. and Jason, who did not participate in the killings. Many of the Rifles, including John Jr. and Jason, were horrified by the killings. When Jason questioned his father about the murders, he stated, "I did not do it, but I approved of it." He told Jason, "God is my judge" and that the circumstances justified their actions.

The Battle of Black Jack

On June 2, 1856, in what is considered by many historians to be the first unofficial battle of the Civil War, John Brown and a small group of his men took on a much larger force of proslavery men at Black Jack, Kansas, located near present-day Baldwin City. In response to the massacre at Pottawatomie, Captain Henry C. Pate led a group of border ruffians on a hunt for Brown and his men. Pate's forces raided the homes of Free State men and took several people captive, including John Jr. and Jason. They were unable to locate Brown, who was hiding out in the woods and preparing an attack.

With only twenty-nine men, Brown led his force into open combat against Pate's force of fifty-five men. The conflict only lasted a few hours. Brown, using strategic tactical maneuvers that made use of the natural landscape, was able to trick the proslavery force into thinking they were outnumbered. Pate surrendered and came to an agreement with Brown, in which both sides would release their captives. The Battle of Black Jack was not a significant military victory and did not end the violence in Kansas, but it was a symbolic victory for the antislavery side and for Brown himself. Brown sent news of his victory to abolitionist papers in the North, which further cemented his reputation as an antislavery warrior.

The Osawatomie Raid

On August 30, 1856, hundreds of ruffians, led by Reverend Martin White and John W. Reid, marched on the abolitionist stronghold of Osawatomie, where Brown and his family lived. The town had been abandoned by many of its residents after an attack earlier in the summer, and those who stayed were aware that they could be targeted at any time. Osawatomie was a known abolitionist stronghold and served as Brown's home and base of operations. After Pottawatomie and Black Jack, John Brown had established himself as a serious threat to proslavery forces. After the events of summer 1856, Brown's notoriety had spread beyond Kansas's borders across the nation. He was a rare figure—a white abolitionist willing to use violence against the slave power.

In late August, a group of Missourians, led by General James Lane and Reverend White, planned to raid several Free State towns, starting with Osawatomie and then on to Topeka and Lawrence. Brown knew they were coming and, as he had at Black Jack, organized a small force to defend the town against a much larger group. He had hoped that the same strategy—using guerrilla tactics and natural defenses—would bring him the same success.

Brown's men had made camp outside of town, but the Missourians beat them there. In the early morning of August 30, Frederick Brown became the first casualty of the Battle of Osawatomie, when he was shot and killed by Reverend White on the outskirts of town. Brown's men received the news and headed to defend the town with a force of around forty men. This time, despite their best efforts, the Free State force was soundly defeated and forced to retreat. Several of Brown's men were wounded and/or taken prisoner, and there were a few casualties. Brown himself was grazed by a bullet, but he managed to escape, as did his sons Jason and John Jr.

The ruffians proceeded to loot and burn the town. As John Brown and Jason looked down on Osawatomie from a safe distance, Brown said, "God sees it. I have only a short time to live—only one death to die, and I will die fighting for this cause. There will be no more peace in this land until slavery is done for. I will give them something else to do than to extend slave territory. I will carry the war into Africa." To Brown, "Africa" was a codename for the slaveholding South. After the battle, which gave him the nickname "Osawatomie Brown," he was ready to bring the fight into the slave states of the South, as he had always planned.

The Secret Six

Not long after Osawatomie, Brown traveled to Boston, where the organized abolitionist movement was strong and its supporters were very wealthy. It was in Boston that Brown met a group of men who would become his main supporters and financial backers, known as the Secret Six. Brown was already acquainted with philanthropist Gerrit Smith, who had sold him his family's property in North Elba. In Boston, he met with Franklin B. Sanborn, the secretary of the Massachusetts State Kansas Committee (one of New England's emigrant societies). Sanborn introduced Brown to two abolitionist ministers—Thomas Wentworth Higginson and Theodore Parker—as well as two other members of the Massachusetts Kansas Committee, Samuel Gridley Howe and George Luther Stearns.

All six men were active abolitionists committed to ending slavery, though some were more radical than others. Howe and Parker formed vigilance committees to protect fugitive slaves. Parker and Higginson took up arms to prevent fugitive recapture. Parker was also a supporter of slave rebellions. Stearns hid a fugitive in his home for a month. Whatever their level of active involvement, they all dedicated time and money to the cause and supported Brown's endeavors, although they were not aware of his Virginia plan until much later.

Planning the Raid

Brown traveled all around New England and into Canada on a fundraising and speaking tour. "Bleeding Kansas" was now a part of the national conversation, especially in the newly formed Republican Party. Brown hoped to capitalize on his own notoriety. The tour was not as successful as he would have liked, especially since he would not divulge the details of his plans for the donations received. He did receive a discounted price for a large shipment of weapons called pikes. A pike is a double-edged Bowie knife attached to the end of a long pole. Brown knew that most of the slaves he planned to free in the South would not know how to use firearms and thought the pike would be an effective weapon for them.

By 1857, Brown had chosen Harpers Ferry as his target. Harpers Ferry was a strategic location, located in the Blue Ridge Mountains between the Potomac and Shenandoah Rivers in Virginia (present-day West Virginia). It was also the location of a federal arsenal established by George Washington in the 1790s. Harpers Ferry would lend itself to Brown's strategy of using the landscape as a natural defense. Additionally, it would allow him access to the government's stockpile of arms and ammunition, and he could destroy anything he couldn't steal for his cause. Proximity to the mountain terrain would allow him and his men to escape and remain hidden.

Brown returned to Kansas in late 1857 to gather recruits for his army and informed them that they would be fighting in Virginia, not in Kansas. The small group of men he was able to recruit then traveled to the base in Tabor, where Brown had been storing the weapons he had acquired, and began their training. In January 1858, Brown visited Frederick Douglass in Rochester, New York, and attempted to recruit him. During this visit, Brown discussed his plan with Douglass, which now included the establishment of a Free State for black citizens in the southern Appalachian Mountains. While with Douglass, Brown drafted the "Provisional Constitution and Ordinances for the People of the United States," which he would later present at a conference in Chatham, Ontario in May 1858.

Chatham had a large, free, black population, many of whom were former slaves. Brown hoped to gain the support of the black community there as well as some volunteers for his army. At the Chatham convention for the "Oppressed People of the United States," Brown presented his constitution and publicly announced his plan to raid plantations from a base in the Blue Ridge Mountains and establish a Free State. The constitution was a direct response to the Supreme Court's decision in the Dred Scott case, in which the court decided that black people—slave or free—were not United States citizens and "have no rights which the white man is bound to respect." The preamble to Brown's constitution referenced the decision directly and stated that slavery is "in utter disregard and violation of those eternal and self-evident truths set forth in our Declaration of Independence." The constitution declared that all people, black and white, were equal citizens. Brown went on to state specifically that the Free State was not to be defined as an attempt to "encourage the overthrow of any State Government … and look to no dissolution of the Union, but simply Amendment and Repeal" of those laws (i.e., legal slavery) that he believed violated the founding principles of the United States.

Prelude to Harpers Ferry

On May 19, 1858, Charles A. Hamilton, a Georgia native who had settled in Kansas, led twenty-five proslavery men in a raid on a Free State settlement near the Marais des Cygnes River. They captured eleven Free State men in the village of Trading Post. Hamilton and his men opened fire on the captives. Five of the men were killed and five others wounded. The attack was a response to Free State victories in the January 1858 territorial election as well as President Buchanan's appointment of a new governor, James Wilson Denver, who was willing to make concessions to the Kansas Free Staters.

The Marais des Cygnes massacre gave Brown the excuse he needed to launch an attack that served as a trial run for the Virginia raid. In December, Brown and twenty of his men attacked several proslavery homesteads in Missouri. They stole horses, wagons, and other supplies, and liberated eleven slaves, who Brown guided to freedom to Canada in the early months of 1859. After Brown's Missouri raid, the violence in Kansas began to subside. While this was not a direct result of Brown's actions and the Kansas government was leaning toward a Free State solution, Brown had successfully created an environment of fear and anxiety among the supporters of slavery in Kansas and Missouri. By the time of Brown's

December raid, the proslavery faction had already started to accept that the battle for control of Kansas was futile.

Preparing for the Raid

By mid-1859, Brown was ready to start implementing the Virginia plan. He rented Kennedy Farm in Maryland under the alias Isaac Smith. The farm, which was 5 miles (8.1 kilometers) from Harpers Ferry, would serve as a base of operations and staging area for the raid. Over the next several months, his recruits and supplies arrived for preparation and training. In any correspondence, weapons and recruits were referred to using code words such as "mining tools" and "freight" for arms and "hands" for recruits. Brown's supplies were delivered via rail to Chambersburg, Pennsylvania, an abolitionist town 40 miles (64.4 km) from Kennedy Farm.

From its earliest incarnation, Brown's plan had always been contingent on the support and active participation of the slaves he planned to free. He believed that the slaves, given their freedom, would be both ready and willing to fight alongside him. Brown's experience with slavery and raiding was limited to Kansas and bordering Missouri, but he had no experience with the institution as it existed in the South. He assumed that the slaves and their white owners would react similarly to an attack. He also assumed that he would be able to enlist black leaders such as Harriet Tubman and Frederick Douglass to his cause.

Douglass, who had previously declined Brown's invitation, agreed to meet with him again in August 1859. Douglass and a companion, ex-slave Shields Green, met with Brown

THE STORMING OF THE ENGINE-HOUSE BY THE UNITED STATES MARINES.—[Sketched by Porte Crayon.]

This illustration depicts the US Army storming the engine house at Harpers Ferry on October 18, 1859, after it was captured by John Brown and his men.

in secret at a quarry in Chambersburg to discuss the plan. At this meeting, Brown revealed to Douglass that the new plan was to attack Harpers Ferry. Douglass was against it, believing that it would be fatal for both the fugitive slaves and Brown's men, and that an attack on the federal government would set back the cause. Douglass again declined to participate, but Shields Green chose to join Brown.

John Brown's Last Stand

At eight o'clock in the evening on October 16, John Brown and his twenty-one men (five black and sixteen white) left Kennedy Farm en route to Harpers Ferry. They reached their destination at around ten o'clock, took several watchmen captive, and cut the telegraph wires. In a very short time, they had cut off all communication and seized control of several of the complex's main buildings, including the armory, the arsenal, and the rifle works that manufactured weapons for the government. Brown told his prisoners, "I want to free all the Negroes in this state. If the citizens interfere with me, I must only burn the town and have blood."

After securing Harpers Ferry, Brown sent some of his men to nearby farms to capture slaveholders and free their slaves. One such farm was owned by Colonel Lewis Washington, George Washington's great-grandnephew. The men took Washington captive, freed his slaves, and (at Brown's specific request) took from him several weapons of historical significance that he had inherited from George Washington. The men brought the prisoners back to the armory where Brown gave the freed slaves pikes and directed them to guard their former masters. Brown told Washington that he had been specifically targeted "for the moral effect it would give our cause having one of your name as a prisoner."

Problems started to arise when the newly liberated slaves did not respond as Brown had always assumed they would.

Having no previous notice of the plan, many were confused as to what was happening and wondered if they were also Brown's prisoners. A white man leading a slave rebellion would have been inconceivable to them, and many ended up fleeing back to their farms out of fear. There was also the very real possibility of violent retribution if they did not succeed, as occurred after the Turner Rebellion. The negative response of the freedmen caused Brown to delay in Harpers Ferry, waiting for news of the insurrection to spread around the countryside (which it did not). Instead of gathering his men and stolen weapons and retreating to the mountains per the original plan, Brown chose to wait for rebel slaves who would never come.

Brown's next mistake came after a train arrived at Harpers Ferry in the early morning hours of October 17. One of the townspeople who had avoided capture stopped the train before it reached the station and warned the conductor about the uprising. In an ironic twist, the first casualty of the attack on Harpers Ferry was a free black man, Heyward Shepherd, who worked as a porter at the rail station. Shepherd was shot by two of Brown's men after he refused to halt at their request.

Brown allowed the train to continue east, which was pointless after having the telegraph wires cut. The conductor notified authorities that a group of armed abolitionists had seized Harpers Ferry and started a slave rebellion. Within a few hours, a group of local proslavery farmers and militias arrived, far outnumbering Brown's small force and cutting off any possible escape routes. Brown took his group of hostages to the engine house. By that afternoon, President

Buchanan ordered the arrival of a group of US Marines, led by Robert E. Lee, the future Confederate general.

In the early hours of October 18, Lee sent a note to Brown at the engine house, requiring his unconditional surrender. Brown refused, and Lee's troops stormed the building. Brown, who suffered sword injuries to his head and shoulder, was gravely wounded and was taken prisoner. Of the twenty-two men that attacked Harpers Ferry, ten died from their wounds, including Brown's sons Oliver and Watson; five (including John Brown) were captured on site; and two others were captured at a later date. Only five men, including Owen Brown, managed to escape.

After years of planning, Brown's Harpers Ferry raid lasted only thirty-six hours and was a complete failure. The raid itself is not what makes Harpers Ferry an important event in American history. John Brown and his works came to represent something at the heart of the national debate over slavery: the question of whether the issue could ever be resolved without bloodshed.

A hand-colored engraving of Brown visiting a black child before his execution

Martyr or Murderer?

Chapter Four

More than anything that had come before, the month and a half between Brown's capture and his execution had the greatest impact on his legacy. John Brown made the most of his incarceration and trial, which became a national news story attracting reporters from all corners of the Union. He turned his time in prison into something of a public relations campaign, using his testimony, prison letters, and interviews as a way to control the narrative and get his message out to the public. In the end, his biggest contribution to the war against slavery was not with weapons, but with words.

Trial and Execution

Brown and the rest of the captured raiders were taken to jail in Charles Town, Virginia to await trial. The authorities moved swiftly because they feared both the lynch mobs descending on Charles Town to enact vigilante justice and the possibility that Brown might escape with the help of abolitionists. Brown's first hearing was scheduled for October 25, and he was charged with murder, inciting a slave rebellion, and treason. The trial began on October 27 and lasted four days.

Brown's opening remarks made it clear that he believed he would not be judged fairly. He told the court, "If you seek my blood, you may have it at any moment, without this mockery of a trial … I am ready for my fate." Brown also rejected his lawyer's attempt at an insanity defense in court. He was aware of the fact that a diagnosis of insanity

This illustration depicts the trial of John Brown in Charles Town, Virginia.

would nullify his life's work, and he was more than willing to die for his cause. On October 31, after less than an hour of deliberation, the jury found Brown guilty of all charges.

In his final address to the court on November 2, Brown gave an eloquent statement in which he declared what he had believed his entire life: that everything he had done was sanctioned by God and the Bible. He invoked the Golden Rule and famously said:

> I believe that to have interfered as I have done—in behalf of His despised poor, was not wrong, but right. Now, if it is deemed necessary that I should forfeit my life for the furtherance of the ends of justice, and mingle my blood further with ... the blood of millions in this slave country whose rights are disregarded by wicked, cruel, and unjust enactments—I submit; so let it be done.

When Brown had finished his remarks, the judge sentenced him to death by hanging, but Brown had accepted his fate long before the sentence was handed down. He had come to believe that it was God's will that he be captured and executed, and that his martyrdom would do more for the cause than anything he accomplished during his life.

Brown went to the gallows on December 2, riding atop his own coffin. Before he was strung up, he handed a message to one of his jailers. This note, which proved to be prophetic, said, "I, John Brown, am now quite certain that the crimes of this guilty land: will never be purged away; but with Blood. I had as I now think vainly flattered myself that without

This illustration shows John Brown climbing the stairs to the gallows before his execution by hanging on December 2, 1859.

very much bloodshed; it might be done." As he went to his death, Brown knew that the Civil War—then more than a year away—was inevitable.

Shaping His Own Legacy

The Virginia authorities unintentionally helped Brown gain sympathy for his cause by allowing him to receive visitors and correspond with the outside world during his incarceration. In the six weeks Brown spent in jail, he received about eight hundred visitors (including many reporters) and wrote hundreds of letters. He was also allowed access to Northern newspapers and writings. This freedom gave Brown a brief window of time before his death to get his message out to the world, and he took full advantage of it. John Brown's correspondence during his short prison term was widely circulated in print and served as a way for Brown to shape his own narrative.

In a letter to "E.B." written November 1, Brown writes that he made a tactical mistake at Harpers Ferry because he "mingled with our prisoners and so far sympathized with them and their families that I neglected my duty in other respects." This is a claim he had made previously when interrogated immediately after the raid, and this portrayed him in a sympathetic light. He goes on to state his long-held belief that God had been guiding him in his actions since Kansas. God meant for him to be captured and, ultimately, to die for the cause:

> You know that Christ once armed Peter. So also in my case I think he put a sword in my hand, and there continued so long as he saw best, and then kindly took it from me … I wish you could know with what cheerfulness I am now wielding the 'sword of the Spirit' on the right hand and on the left … God will surely attend to his own cause in the best possible way and time, and he will not forget the work of his own hands.

Brown also wrote to a Reverend McFarland on November 23. Abolitionists had long argued that one could not be both Christian and proslavery, and as his execution date approached, he asked McFarland for spiritual guidance: "There are no ministers of Christ here. These ministers who profess to be Christian, and hold slaves or advocate slavery,

I cannot abide them. My knees will not bend in prayer with them while their hands are stained with the blood of souls." He went on to equate himself with Paul the Apostle, who was also imprisoned and martyred. "I think I feel as happy as Paul did when he lay in prison," Brown wrote. "He knew if they killed him it would greatly advance the cause of Christ … Let them hang me; I forgive them, and may God forgive them, for they know not what they do."

Brown stated that he has no regrets for defying the laws of man because Christ told him to "remember them that are in bonds, as bound with them, and to do towards them as I would wish them to do towards me." His only regret, he said, was for his wife and children, but he remained confident that "God will be a husband to the widow, and a father to the fatherless." In this and many more of Brown's letters, his only worry was related to his family and how they would move on after his death. He asked many of his supporters if they would help to care for Mary and his remaining children, financially or otherwise, after his execution.

By all accounts—both his own and those of the people who encountered him during his imprisonment—Brown was perfectly content. He had accepted his fate, and in many of his letters, he goes out of his way to assure family, friends, and other supporters that he was in good spirits and looked after well in prison. He had an especially good relationship with his jailer, John Avis, who also happened to be one of the militia captains sent to put down Brown's raid. Brown wrote to his wife, Mary, on October 31, "You may rest assured that both kind hearts and kind faces are more or less about me whilst thousands are thirsting for

This painting, *The Last Moments of John Brown*, by Thomas Hovenden, depicts John Brown kissing a young slave child on his way to the gallows. Even though this story is most likely untrue, it was widely accepted and perpetuated by those sympathetic to Brown.

my blood." On November 4, he wrote to abolitionist Lydia Maria Child, who had offered to come visit him, to assure her that he was fine and her energies were better spent helping his family. Regarding Avis, Brown wrote, "I am in [the] charge of a most humane gentleman who with his family have rendered me every possible attention I have desired."

Brown wrote a letter addressed to his entire family on November 30, two days before his execution. Knowing this would be his last letter to them, he beseeched his children to put their faith in God and to "abhor with undying hatred … that sum of all villainies, Slavery." He assures his family that he is "writing the hour of my public murder with great composure of mind, & cheerfulness; feeling the strongest assurance that in no other possible way could I be used to so much advance the cause of God; & of humanity; & that nothing that either I or my family have sacrificed or suffered will be lost."

Once Brown's trial statements and prison letters were circulated in the North, many changed their view of the man. His words did not read like the ramblings of an insane person. They painted a picture of a man who was deeply committed to his family, to God, and to fighting the evils of slavery at any cost. Many people who had initially disavowed him started to see Brown as a sympathetic, heroic, and even Christlike figure.

Calls for Secession

Brown had long been notorious as a thief and a murderer to proslavery people in Kansas and Missouri. After Harpers Ferry, this sentiment spread to every corner of the slaveholding South. The Southern response to the raid was to view Brown as a representative of the larger antislavery movement, including the "Black Republican" party. This fueled the existing panic about widespread insurrections, attacks by militant abolitionists, and the election of an antislavery government that would destroy the Southern economy and diminish its political power. There were some radicals in the South, known as fire-eaters, who had been calling for secession since the early 1850s. After Brown's raid, many more Southerners came to believe that the only way to maintain their way of life—and the slave system—was to secede from the Union.

By all laws of the United States of America, slavery was legal, and the slaveholders had every right to their life, liberty, and property. The facts were not up for debate: John Brown was a thief and a murderer. He killed innocent people and terrorized the region, stole their property (human, animal, and otherwise), and had as yet gone unpunished. Southerners believed that Brown had the full support and financial backing of Northern politicians and abolitionist organizations, and his actions in Kansas and the Harpers Ferry raid were widely considered to be acts of war against the South.

Southern newspapers openly called for secession after Harpers Ferry. On October 25, an editorial in the *Richmond Enquirer* openly called for disunion. Harpers Ferry, it claimed,

> has rallied to that standard men who formerly looked upon [disunion] with horror; it has revived, with ten-fold strength, the desire

of a Southern Confederacy. The heretofore most determined friends of the Union may now be heard saying, 'if under the form of a Confederacy our peace is disturbed, our State invaded, its peaceful citizens cruelly murdered by those who should be our warmest friends… and the people of the North sustain the outrage, Then let disunion come.'

A November 7 editorial in the *Charleston Mercury* takes an equally strong stance, stating that the time had come to separate from the North. The editorial took the view that the Constitution had been violated and that the Union, as it stood, provided no security for the life or property of southern people. It warned the people, "emissaries are in our midst, sent here by a party which claims to have the good of the country at heart, but in fact are assassins." For this author, the time for compromise was over: "The curtain falls, and the Republic framed by the hands of Washington and Jefferson fades from view. Better civil war than injustice and oppression."

John Brown had no affiliation with any political party and was not a member of any organizations. The fact that he had received support and funds from a very small group of abolitionists was enough to convince the South that he was an instrument of a Northern conspiracy. While Brown was viewed as a dishonorable, treasonous, murdering thief for openly violating southerners' constitutional rights, they agreed with him on one thing: war was inevitable.

Conflicted Proslavery Southerners

Many of those who had personal experience and firsthand encounters with Brown after the raid came away with respect for him despite his crimes. Governor Henry Wise had been with Brown since shortly after his capture, and in that time, he formed a surprising opinion of the man who would be convicted of treason against his state:

> … a bundle of the best nerves I ever saw cut and thrust and bleeding and in bonds. He is a man of clear head, of courage, fortitude and simple ingenuousness. He is cool, collected, and indomitable, and it is but just to him to say, that he was humane to his prisoners … and he inspired me with great trust in his integrity, as a man of truth. He is a fanatic, vain, and garrulous, but firm, truthful, and intelligent.

Even though Wise clearly respected Brown, he in no uncertain terms believed that Brown and his men were "murderers, traitors, robbers, insurrectionists," and "wanton, malicious, unprovoked felons." Governor Wise admired Brown's strength and courage, but Brown's actions were, in Wise's mind and those of all proslavery Southerners, unequivocally evil.

Congressman Clement Vallandigham, a proslavery Democrat from Ohio who was present during Brown's interrogation immediately after Harpers Ferry, had a similar view of the man. Vallandigham believed that Brown was "as brave and resolute a man as ever headed an insurrection" and would have made a great leader had he been working toward "a good cause." He went on to say that Brown was "the farthest possible remove from the ordinary ruffian, fanatic, or madman" and that Harpers Ferry was "one of the best planned and executed conspiracies that ever failed."

Wise was faced with the decision of Brown's sentence and, because of his political ambitions and his Southern constituents' thirst for Brown's blood, he had no choice but to execute him, even though he had come to respect the man. Facts were facts: Brown was guilty and the punishment for his crimes was execution by hanging. In his December 5 message to the Virginia Legislature, Wise presented a lengthy explanation of his decision. He stated the crimes of Brown and his men: disturbing the peace, kidnapping, robbery, murder, and violation of property. He also expressed the common opinion that Brown was not working alone but placed part of the blame on the abolitionist movement and the North as a whole. Wise stated, "An evil spirit of fanaticism has seized upon negro slavery as the one object of social reform and the one idea of its abolition has seemed to madden whole masses of one entire section of the country."

Wise believed it was the right decision to execute Brown, even though it would likely turn him into a martyr for the cause. Anything less would give impunity to those "fanatics" who would "[set] up their individual supremacy over law, life, property, and civil liberty itself." Wise asked the legislature, "What is this but anarchy ... and the overthrow of all rights, of all property, of all government, of all religion, of all rule among men?" It had become clear to Wise that battle lines

This 1859 broadside is sympathetic to Brown and calls for all Christians to pray for him ahead of his execution for treason.

Martyr or Murderer?

between the North and South were already drawn, and he acknowledged in his closing remarks that "the present relations between the states cannot be permitted longer to exist without abolishing slavery throughout the United States, or compelling us to defend it by arms." Like Brown, Wise knew that the nation had reached the point where armed conflict to determine the fate of American slavery was unavoidable.

The Republican Party Response

With the 1860 election just months away, the Republican Party and its supporters completely disavowed John Brown. The Democrats had already popularized the term "Black Republicans" for the party, which was opposed to the spread of slavery in the territories. This strategy exploited the rampant racism and economic anxiety of whites by associating the Republicans as the black people's party and claiming that their ultimate goal was to elevate slaves and free blacks above whites.

Brown's actions were a major liability for the Republican Party and their candidate, Abraham Lincoln. In a February 1860 speech called the Cooper Union Address, Lincoln directly addressed Southern claims that the Republicans were militant abolitionists who supported slave rebellion: "You charge that we stir up insurrections among your slaves. We deny it; and what is your proof? Harper's Ferry! John Brown!! John Brown was no Republican." He went on to call Brown's raid "peculiar" and "absurd" and likened Brown to "an enthusiast [who] broods over the oppression of a people till he fancies himself commissioned by Heaven to liberate them." Lincoln, like many others who did not want to be associated with Brown's violent tactics, dismissed him as a religious fanatic.

The Work of a Madman

The initial response to Brown's raid among even the staunchest of Northern abolitionists was not supportive. They denied the Southern claim that Brown was representative of their movement and instead dismissed him as a fanatic and a lone wolf. The latter claim was not without merit, since Brown was never involved with the organized movement (except to solicit funds) and took a militant stance that was not shared by the majority of American abolitionists, especially the white ones.

Soon after the raid, two of the most influential antislavery publishers in the North, William Lloyd Garrison and Horace Greeley, published articles that claimed Brown was insane. In the *Liberator*, Garrison wrote that Brown's raid was "a misguided, wild, and apparently insane, though disinterested and well intended effort." In the *New-York Tribune*, Greeley wrote that Harpers Ferry was "the work of a madman" and suggested that Brown's time in Kansas had driven him insane.

An editorial published in the *Boston Transcript* on November 4 dismisses the entire event as "a most foolish, impracticable and unfortunate scheme, planned and lead on by a brave, simple-hearted, unselfish, and modest monomaniac." It advises the "wise men at the South" to disregard Brown as someone who has been "touched by insanity" and cautions that, whatever his "guilt or folly," to convict an insane man "will be the most terrible fruit slavery has ever borne, and will excite the condemnation of the entire civilized world."

Brown had rejected an insanity defense at his trial, but in the initial aftermath of the raid, the insanity angle was a common strategy used by antislavery Northerners to rationalize Brown's actions and distance themselves from the man who was now the nation's most notorious abolitionist. No one wished to distance themselves from Brown more than the Secret Six, who feared indictment as co-conspirators. Once Brown's papers were discovered during the post-raid investigation of Kennedy Farm, correspondence with members of the Secret Six and others was published in Northern newspapers.

Gerrit Smith had a mental breakdown and checked himself into an asylum. Sanborn, Howe, and Stearns went into hiding in Canada for several months. Frederick Douglass was also implicated and left for Canada and on to England shortly after the raid. From there, he sent a letter to be published in Northern papers stating that he had no involvement in Harpers Ferry. Of Brown's main supporters, only Thomas Wentworth Higginson and Theodore Parker publicly defended him.

There were some in the North who, very early on, realized that Brown was of more use to the abolitionists' cause dead than alive. One such man was Reverend Henry Ward Beecher, the brother of author Harriet Beecher Stowe. Beecher was a lifelong abolitionist who had raised funds to send Sharps rifles to emigrants in Kansas during the territorial crisis. These weapons became widely known as "Beecher's Bibles" after he made the claim that "there was more moral power in one of those instruments, so far as the slaveholders of Kansas were concerned, than in a hundred Bibles." On October 30, Beecher preached a sermon in which he advised his congregants, "Let no man pray that Brown be spared. Let Virginia make him a martyr … His soul was noble; his work miserable. But [his execution] would redeem all that, and round up Brown's failure with heroic success." Beecher understood, as Brown himself did, that his death would do more for the cause than any acquittal or reduced sentence on the basis of an insanity defense.

The Transcendentalists

During his fundraising tour of New England in the years before the raid, Brown had impressed several of the most influential literary figures of the age—the Transcendentalists. Men like Henry David Thoreau and Ralph Waldo Emerson listened to Brown speak in Concord, Massachusetts, and invited him to dine in their homes. These men were impressed by Brown and became critical to shaping his legacy in the aftermath of Harpers Ferry.

Henry David Thoreau was one of the first public supporters of Brown after the raid. Thoreau was well known for his essay "Civil Disobedience," which was inspired by the Mexican-American War and his hatred of slavery. In it, he argues that an individual is obligated to act according to their moral principles and disobey the government laws if they are unjust. In this respect, Thoreau's beliefs aligned with Brown's. On October 30, Thoreau gave a speech, later published as "A Plea for Captain John Brown," in which he refuted all claims of Brown's insanity. Thoreau chastised antislavery editors and Republican politicians for their cowardice and accused them of not supporting Brown because it would lose them subscribers and voters.

Thoreau praised Brown as a man of faith and religious principles who gave his life to the cause of the oppressed even though it did not personally affect him. To Thoreau, Brown was the greatest of all American heroes:

> He did not value his bodily life in comparison with ideal things. He did not recognize unjust human laws, but resisted them as he was bid ... No man in America has ever stood up so persistently or effectively for the dignity of human nature, knowing himself for a man, and the equal of any and all governments. In that sense he was the most American of us all.

He went on to explicitly compare Brown's execution to the crucifixion of Jesus Christ, which he called "the two ends of a chain which is not without its links. He is not Old Brown any longer; he is an angel of light."

Ralph Waldo Emerson also came out in support of Brown. Emerson, who was the nation's most prominent intellectual at the time, gave a speech in Boston on November 8. He echoed the Christ comparison, referring to Brown as "that new saint, than whom none purer or more brave was ever led by love of men into conflict and death,—the new saint awaiting his martyrdom, and who, if he shall suffer, will make the gallows glorious like the cross." This concept of Brown as a Christlike martyr, defended by the

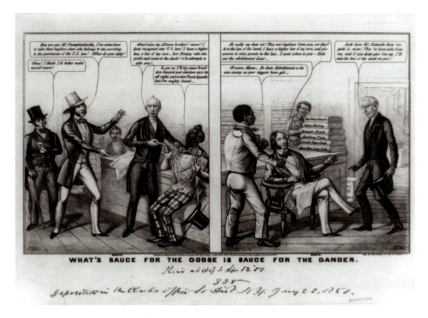

This pro-Southern political cartoon criticizes Northern abolitionists opposed to the Fugitive Slave Act of 1850 and calls for the seizure of Northern goods as retaliation for their freeing slaves.

Transcendentalists, soon became popular among Northern abolitionists, who came to realize that Brown's martyrdom could serve their cause.

The Tide Turns in the North

William Lloyd Garrison, arguably the most influential mainstream abolitionist of the time, had always been a pacifist. Like so many others, he initially dismissed Brown as insane, but he soon came around on the issue. Two weeks after Brown's execution, the view of John Brown as an abolitionist martyr had taken hold in the North. Garrison published an editorial in the December 16 issue of the *Liberator* in which he honored Brown and demonstrated an uncharacteristically militant approach.

Martyr or Murderer?

Garrison claimed that Brown's trial was a mockery and that he was "judicially assassinated." He stated that Brown's actions were justified and reminded his readers that "God knows nothing of color or complexion." Garrison advised them that if they believed in freedom for people of their own race then they must "cover, not only with a mantle of charity, but with the admiration of [their] hearts, the effort of John Brown at Harpers Ferry."

He went on to state that, though he remained committed to peace, he did not believe it compromised his position to wish success to slave insurrections in the South. He stated plainly that, "rather than see men wear their chains in a cowardly and servile spirit, I would, as an advocate of peace, much rather see them breaking the head of the tyrant with their chains."

John Brown in Popular Culture

After his execution, Brown became immortalized in poetry, plays, and songs—both in the North and in the South. The Northern works portrayed Brown as a hero, and the Southern works portrayed him as a villain. If he was Christlike in the North, he was satanic in the South. One popular Southern song, "John Brown's Entry into Hell," written in 1863, tells the tale of John Brown's arrival in Hell after his execution.

An early verse describes Brown being welcomed by Satan himself: "Brown to receive they now prepare / All eager in the joy to share / Old Satan from his throne came down / And left his seat for Old John Brown." Satan tells Brown, "As oft you've murdered, lied and stole / It did rejoice my burning soul." He also informs Brown, "Old Abraham [Lincoln] is coming too," and goes on to detail a number of abolitionists who are also destined for Hell. The song ends:

> And now, O! John, on earth oppress'd,
> You are with us a welcome guest;
> On earth you played our part full well,
> So now with us forever dwell.

In this and other popular works in Southern culture, Brown was demonized. In the North, the opposite was true. Ralph Waldo Emerson first popularized the idea of Brown's martyrdom with his statement about the "gallows glorious," and Northern poetry dealt largely with Christlike comparisons. One poem made a direct comparison between Brown and Christ:

> For as that cross of shame
> Forever thence became
> Earth's holiest shrine;
> So must this gallows tree,
> Redeemed from infamy
> Become for bond and free
> A sacred sign.

Brown was the subject of a song popular with Union soldiers during the Civil War. "John Brown's Body" evolved from an old folk hymn but became a popular marching song for Union forces after the lyrics were changed to be about

Martyr or Murderer?

Brown. The song, excerpted below, portrays Brown as an American hero and Christlike figure.

> John Brown's body lies a-mouldering in the grave,
> While weep the sons of bondage, whom he
>   ventured all to save,
> But tho' he lost his life in struggling for the slave,
> His soul is marching on.
>
> John Brown was a hero undaunted, true, and brave,
> And Kansas knew his valor, when he fought her
>   rights to save:
> And now thought the grass grows green above
>   his grave,
> His soul is marching on.
>
> John Brown was John the Baptist, of Christ we
>   are to see,
> Christ who of the bondman shall the Liberator be,
> And soon throughout the sunny South, the
>   slaves shall be set free,
> For his soul is marching on.

"John Brown's Body" became the basis for another famous Civil War song, "The Battle Hymn of the Republic," written by Julia Ward Howe, wife of Secret Six member Samuel Howe.

Black Americans' Response

While white America had varying reactions to John Brown, the reaction from black America was overwhelmingly positive. John Brown was a hero to the black community. He was the only white person in the nation willing to give his life for their freedom. Brown had always fully believed in racial equality, was free of racial prejudice, and practiced what he preached in his own life.

During Brown's imprisonment, a group of black women raised funds to help support his wife and family in North Elba. On the day of his execution and after, black communities throughout the North held services and went into mourning for Brown, which included closing local businesses. Prominent black leaders openly supported Brown—something even his closest white backers did not dare do.

Ohio abolitionist Charles H. Langston published a letter praising Brown in the November 18 edition of the *Cleveland Plain Dealer*. Langston's letter stated that Brown's actions at Harpers Ferry were justified by the Bible. Brown had gone into Virginia to help the slaves and "let the oppressed go free." He also went to "put to death … those who steal men and sell them, and in whose hands stolen men are found." Langston believed, as did Brown, that his action were in line with the "plain teaching of the word of God."

Langston eulogized Brown at a memorial service held in Cleveland. He stated, "I never thought that I should ever join in doing honor to or mourning for any American white man," and yet he did just that. Langston honored Brown who, alone among white Americans, "fully, really and actively believed in equality and brotherhood." Langston declared that Brown was "the only American citizen who has lived fully up to the Declaration of Independence." His was a

The Oberlin Rescuers in 1859. Charles H. Langston is pictured near the middle, holding a hat to his chest.

sentiment shared by the majority of black Americans, who felt that John Brown truly saw them as his equal.

John Brown's contemporaries were divided on the question of whether he was a hero or a villain. From a historical standpoint, it is easy to view Brown in a sympathetic light. During the Civil War, hundreds of thousands of Union soldiers took up arms against supporters of slavery. History considers them heroic because of it. Brown was always on the right side of history when it came to slavery, which is unquestionably a moral evil. At the time, slavery was the law of the land, and those who supported it naturally viewed Brown as a treasonous criminal and a terrorist. The question at the heart of the matter remains: Do positive ends justify violent means? It is a question we are still asking ourselves today, and there is no easy answer.

Nat Turner Rebellion

Enslaved preacher Nat Turner was one of John Brown's greatest inspirations. On August 21, 1831, Turner led a slave rebellion in Southampton County, Virginia. Like Brown, Turner was deeply religious and believed that he had been given a sign from God to attack the institution of slavery through violence. Turner and his men killed the family of Turner's master, Joseph Travis. They then proceeded to go on a killing spree throughout the county, gathering more followers along the way. By the end of the rebellion, Turner's men numbered about sixty, and they had killed fifty-five white Southerners.

Like Brown, Turner was variously viewed as a hero, a villain, and an insane religious fanatic. Also like Brown, Turner became an iconic figure to black Americans, especially during the Jim Crow era and the civil rights movement of the 1960s. The black-led Turner Rebellion did not galvanize the abolitionist movement in the same way that the white-led Brown rebellion did. Abolitionists, even those who had long preached nonviolence, martyred Brown and used the situation to their advantage. The Turner Rebellion presented them with a similar opportunity years earlier, but the mainstream movement did not seize it. A combination

This illustration depicts Nat Turner and his men planning the August 1831 slave rebellion that would later inspire John Brown.

of Turner's race and slave status and the fact that, in 1831, the abolitionist movement was in its infancy, led to disparate outcomes. The immediate effects of the Turner Rebellion were harsher slave codes and widespread violent retribution toward slaves. The Brown rebellion, on the other hand, brought the nation one step closer to the Civil War and abolition of slavery in America.

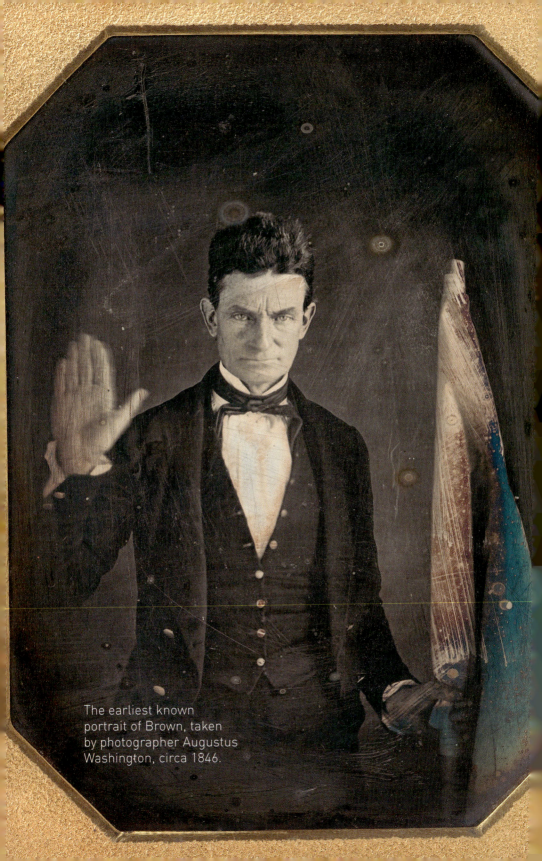

The earliest known portrait of Brown, taken by photographer Augustus Washington, circa 1846.

His Soul Marches On

Chapter Five

The concept of terrorism in the modern world is much different than it was in the antebellum South when John Brown was using violent tactics to overthrow slavery. In Brown's time, battles were fought in close combat with Bowie knives and single-shot rifles. Today, the rules of engagement are much different. Mass casualties and collateral damage are accepted and even preferred by modern terrorists. The basic definition of a terrorist— a person who uses violence and intimidation, especially against civilians, in the pursuit of political aims—still applies to Brown. Some modern terrorists have claimed him as inspiration, but he has also inspired a new generation of American heroes: civil rights activists forced to fight for racial equality long after the abolition of American slavery.

Storer College

John Brown, like his father before him, had always been a proponent of equal educational opportunities for black students. The post–Civil War Reconstruction years saw the establishment of several colleges with the goal of providing educational opportunities for black Americans. The founding of these institutions was one of the main goals of the Freedmen's Bureau, a government organization created after the war to assist former slaves. One such school, Storer College, was founded in 1867 in Harpers Ferry, just a few miles away from the site of Brown's historic raid. Storer was founded as a normal school for training teachers and was one of the first institutions in the United States open to students of all races, genders, and religions.

Harpers Ferry held a special significance for the black community and was inextricably linked with John Brown. In 1881, Storer trustee Frederick Douglass gave a speech about Brown at the college. Douglass's stated purpose of his John Brown speech was "to pay a just debt long due" and "to vindicate in some degree a great historical character." Douglass did not excuse Brown's violent actions but placed them in their proper context. Brown's acts of violence, Douglass claimed, were a direct response to the violence of slavery and the slave trade, which were "far more cruel and bloody" than anything Brown had done. In placing Brown's actions in historical context, Douglass hoped that "which time has done for other great men of his class, that will time certainly do for John Brown." The speech was later printed and the proceeds for its sale went to the establishment of a John Brown Professorship at Storer.

Three students sit on the lawn at Storer College in Harpers Ferry, Virginia. The campus was located a short distance from the site of John Brown's raid.

The Niagara Movement and the NAACP

Brown's legacy became even more important to black Americans in the years following the end of Reconstruction, which saw increased discrimination and violence against them. Black Americans suffered severe violations of their civil liberties as a result of legalized discrimination in the form of Jim Crow laws. They were subject to segregation, disenfranchisement (discriminatory voting laws), and lynching (the illegal mob murder of an accused criminal without a trial). In response, some black leaders looked to Brown for inspiration in their continued fight for equal civil rights.

One of the most influential black activists of the time, W. E. B. Du Bois, organized the Niagara Movement in 1905. The second conference of this civil rights organization—which would become the National Association for the Advancement of Colored People (NAACP)—occurred at Storer College in 1906. Du Bois purposefully chose Harpers Ferry as the location for this historic meeting and stated in his address, "Here on the scene of John Brown's martyrdom, we reconsecrate ourselves, our honor, and our property to the final emancipation of the race which John Brown died to make free."

The NAACP was formally established in 1909, and many of the organization's founders credited Brown as an inspiration. In 1932, the organization attempted to place a tablet commemorating Brown on the Storer College campus. At the ceremony, NAACP member and founder of the John

A tablet honoring John Brown is placed at the location of the former Storer College by members of the NAACP in 2006. NAACP members had been attempting to honor Brown with this tablet since the 1930s.

Brown Memorial Association, J. Max Barber, stated that the NAACP was dedicated to carrying on Brown's ideals and that the organization was "a direct descendant of the old League of Gileadites … John Brown should be an inspiration to you in your fight for justice and self-respect." The college administrators did not allow the tablet to be placed, claiming its text was too militant, and it was moved to the NAACP office in New York. Storer College, which closed in 1955, was taken over by the National Parks Service (NPS). In 2006, the NPS invited the NAACP to place the tablet on site, where it was always meant to be.

Twentieth-Century Domestic Terrorism

While Brown served as an inspiration for many black leaders in their fight for racial equality, he also inspired many of the nation's most notorious domestic terrorists. In the late twentieth century, anti-abortion activists committed acts of violence against clinics that provided abortion services. Their tactics included harassment, burglaries, bombings, and the murder of abortion providers. John Burt, who was convicted for his role in several attacks on clinics in Florida in the 1980s, is one of the perpetrators who claimed Brown as inspiration. Burt stated that, "maybe like Harpers Ferry, where John Brown used violence to bring the evils of slavery into focus, these bombings may do the same thing on the abortion issue."

Paul Hill, who was an associate of Burt's, was convicted of the 1994 murder of abortion provider Dr. John Britton and his bodyguard, James Barrett. Hill also credited Brown as an inspiration. Like Brown, Hill claimed that he was doing God's bidding. He stated in a letter from prison that Brown was a source of encouragement to him. Not long before he was executed for his crimes, Hill wrote, "the political impact of Brown's actions continues to serve as a powerful paradigm in my understanding of the potential effects the use of defensive force may have for the unborn."

Timothy McVeigh, who perpetrated the 1995 bombing of the Alfred P. Murrah Federal Building in Oklahoma City, has also been linked to Brown. During McVeigh's incarceration, journalist Dan Herbeck reported that Brown

The wreckage of the Albert P. Murrah Federal Building in Oklahoma City after it was bombed by Timothy McVeigh in 1995

was one of McVeigh's heroes. Like Brown, McVeigh chose a federal building as the site of his attack. McVeigh's attack was motivated by his anger at the federal government in the aftermath of incidents in Ruby Ridge, Idaho, and Waco, Texas. In both cases, the federal government engaged in deadly confrontations at the compounds of individuals who the government claimed were illegally selling weapons. A gun enthusiast, McVeigh saw these attacks as the federal government interfering with the Second Amendment rights of US citizens.

There are parallels to Brown in all these cases. Burt and Hill claimed to be acting in God's name against abortion, a legal procedure, which they viewed as a sin. McVeigh targeted the federal government for what he viewed as its violation of the civil rights of Americans. All used terrorist tactics to further their political goals, and all murdered innocent people in the process.

It is indisputable that John Brown was a criminal and a murderer, but how one views him really depends on one's perspective. During Brown's time, he was a villain to those who supported slavery, a hero and a savior to the black citizens he died for, and a complicated figure to those who were against the spread of slavery but did not support the use of violence. Political motivations were also a factor in how people responded to Brown. If it did not benefit one's cause to support Brown—as with the Republicans running for office or the abolitionists who did not want to be associated with his crimes—he was an insane fanatic. As America moved closer to war, and a martyr was needed for the movement, Brown became a Christlike figure. In this respect, the question of whether Brown was a hero or a villain is completely subjective.

Today, over a century removed as we are from the institution of slavery, it is easier to view Brown in a positive light. His actions at Harpers Ferry were one of the final sparks that led to the war that ultimately freed the slaves. Slavery is a stain on American history, and anyone who fought against it ended up on the right side of history. It is important to understand Brown's actions in their historical context to see the entire picture of the man who some consider one of the nation's greatest heroes and others consider America's first terrorist.

agrarian society A society in which the economy is based on agricultural production.

annexation Incorporating new territory into an existing country.

appropriations bill An act of a legislature authorizing money to be paid from the treasury for a specific use.

arsenal A collection of weapons and military equipment stored by a country, person, or group.

border ruffians Proslavery Missouri residents who crossed into Kansas Territory to commit voter fraud and acts of violence.

Bowie knife A stout, single-edged hunting knife with part of the back edge curved concavely to a point and sharpened.

Calvinism A Christian theology stressing the depravity of humans as born sinners, the sovereignty of God, the doctrine of predestination, and the supreme authority of the Bible.

disenfranchisement The state of being deprived of a right or privilege, especially the right to vote.

Glossary

emigrant aid company An organization that helped relocate abolitionists to Kansas Territory to ensure it would become a Free State.

fire-eaters A group of radical proslavery Southerners who advocated for secession from the Union over a decade before the start of the Civil War.

gallows A structure used to execute criminals by hanging.

lynching To put to death, especially by hanging, by mob action and without legal authority.

manifest destiny The nineteenth-century belief that the expansion of the United States throughout North America was both justified and ordained by God.

militia An armed force of civilians.

moral suasion A tactic used by abolitionists of appealing to someone's morality as a way to get them to change their beliefs and/or behavior.

normal school A school or college for the training of teachers.

pike A weapon composed of a double-sided knife attached to the end of a spear.

1800
John Brown born in Torrington, Connecticut, to Owen and Ruth Mills Brown.

1812
Twelve-year-old Brown witnesses a slave child being beaten.

1831
Nat Turner leads a slave rebellion in Southampton County, Virginia.

1837
Abolitionist Elijah P. Lovejoy is murdered in Alton, Illinois; John Brown pledges himself to the abolition of slavery.

1847
Brown meets Frederick Douglass.

Chronology

1848
Brown acquires land from Gerrit Smith in North Elba, New York, and pledges to help the black community there; the United States acquires the Mexican Cession territory when the Treaty of Guadalupe Hidalgo ends the Mexican-American War.

1850
The Compromise of 1850, including the Fugitive Slave Law, is passed.

1851
Brown forms the United States League of Gileadites in response to the fugitive slave laws.

1854
The Kansas-Nebraska Act is passed, opening the territory for settlement; Brown's sons Owen, Frederick, and Salmon found Brown's Station near Osawatomie.

Books

Earle, Jonathan. *John Brown's Raid on Harpers Ferry: A Brief History with Documents.* Boston, MA: Bedford/St. Martin's, 2008.

Etcheson, Nicole. *Bleeding Kansas: Contested Liberty in the Civil War Era.* Lawrence, KS: University Press of Kansas, 2004.

Ferrell, Claudine L. *The Abolitionist Movement.* Westport, CT: Greenwood Press, 2006.

Horwitz, Tony. *Midnight Rising: John Brown and the Raid That Sparked the Civil War.* New York: Holt, 2011.

Schraff, Anne E. *John Brown: We Came to Free the Slaves.* Berkeley Heights, NJ: Enslow Publishers, 2010.

Stefoff, Rebecca. *John Brown and the Armed Resistance to Slavery.* New York: Cavendish Square Publishing, 2016.

Further Information

Websites

"Africans in America"
https://www.pbs.org/wgbh/aia/home.html
This site goes more in depth about slavery in America.

American Experience: "The Abolitionists"
https://ny.pbslearningmedia.org/collection/abolitionists/
This site contains video portrayals of famous abolitionists.

"Civil War on the Western Border"
http://www.civilwaronthewesternborder.org/
This has more information pertaining to Kansas City during the Civil War.

"John Brown: Hero or Terrorist?"
http://www.digitalhistory.uh.edu/active_learning/explorations/brown/john_brown_menu.cfm
This site offers further analysis about John Brown.

"John Brown: The Abolitionist & His Legacy"
https://www.gilderlehrman.org/sites/default/files/swf/jbrown/index.html
This is a slideshow all about John Brown.

Carton, Evan. *Patriotic Treason: John Brown and the Soul of America*. New York. Free Press, 2006.

Decaro, Louis A., Jr. *"Fire from the Midst of You": A Religious Life of John Brown*. New York: New York University Press, 2002.

Donahue, James J. "Hardly the Voice of the Same Man": "Civil Disobedience" and "Thoreau's Response to John Brown," *Midwest Quarterly* 48:2 (Winter 2007), p. 247.

Earle, Jonathan, ed. *John Brown's Raid on Harpers Ferry: A Brief History with Documents*. Boston, MA: Bedford/St. Martin's, 2008.

Earle, Jonathan, and Diane Mutti Burke, eds. *Bleeding Kansas, Bleeding Missouri: The Long Civil War on the Border*. Lawrence, KS: University Press of Kansas, 2013.

Etcheson, Nicole. *Bleeding Kansas: Contested Liberty in the Civil War Era*. Lawrence, KS: University Press of Kansas, 2004.

Selected Bibliography

Ferrell, Claudine L. *The Abolitionist Movement.* Westport, CT: Greenwood Press, 2006.

Gilpin, R. Blakeslee. *John Brown Still Lives! America's Long Reckoning With Violence, Equality, and Change.* Chapel Hill, NC: University of North Carolina Press, 2011.

Goodrich, Thomas. *War to the Knife: Bleeding Kansas, 1854–1861.* Mechanicsburg, PA: Stackpole Books, 1998.

Horwitz, Tony. *Midnight Rising: John Brown and the Raid That Sparked the Civil War.* New York: Holt, 2011.

Marrin, Albert. *A Volcano Beneath the Snow: John Brown's War Against Slavery.* New York: Alfred A. Knopf, 2014.

McGlone, Robert. *John Brown's War Against Slavery.* New York: Cambridge University Press, 2009.

Morretta, Alison. *Legal Debates of the Antislavery Movement.* New York: Cavendish Square Publishing, 2016.

Oates, Stephen. *To Purge This Land with Blood: A Biography of John Brown.* Amherst, MA: University of Massachusetts Press, 1984.

Paz, Franco A., "The Uprisings of Nat Turner and John Brown: Response and Treatment from the Abolitionist Movement and the Press." *Inquiries Journal/Student Pulse* 8:5 (2016). http://www.inquiriesjournal.com/a?id=1409.

Potter, David M. *The Impending Crisis: America Before the Civil War, 1848–1861.* New York: Harper Perennial, 2011.

Renehan, Edward J., Jr. *The Secret Six: The True Tale of the Men Who Conspired with John Brown.* New York: Crown Publishers, 1995.

Reynolds, David S. *John Brown, Abolitionist: The Man Who Killed Slavery, Sparked the Civil War, and Seeded Civil Rights.* New York: Vintage Books, 2005.

Russo, Peggy, and Paul Finkelman, eds. *Terrible Swift Sword: The Legacy of John Brown.* Athens, OH: Ohio University Press, 2005.

Schraff, Anne E. *John Brown: We Came to Free the Slaves.* Berkeley Heights, NJ: Enslow Publishers, 2010.

Stauffer, John, and Zoe Trodd, eds. *The Tribunal: Responses to John Brown and the Harpers Ferry Raid*. Cambridge, MA: Harvard University Press, 2012.

Stefoff, Rebecca. *John Brown and the Armed Resistance to Slavery*. New York, NY: Cavendish Square Publishing, 2016.

Sutton, Robert K. *Stark Mad Abolitionists: Lawrence, Kansas, and the Battle Over Slavery in the Civil War Era*. New York: Skyhorse Publishing, 2017.

Waugh, John C. *On the Brink of Civil War: The Compromise of 1850 and How It Changed the Course of American History*. Lanham, MD: Rowman & Littlefield Publishers, 2003.

Williams, Heather Andrea. *American Slavery: A Very Short Introduction*. New York: Oxford University Press, 2014.

Page numbers in **boldface** are illustrations.

abolition, 5–6, 12, 15, 22, 74, 91
abolitionist, 5, 8–9, 11–13, 20, 22–23, 29, 31, 33–34, 40, 42–44, 46–48, 51, 53, 57, 60, 64, 67, 70–72, 74, 76–78, 81, 83, 85, 88–89, 98
agrarian society, 19
American Revolution, the, 6, 15
annexation, 23, 26
appropriations bill, 26
arsenal, 54, 59

Battle of Black Jack, the, 50–52
Beecher, Reverend Henry Ward, 78–79
Bleeding Kansas, **32**, **49**, 54
border ruffians, 33
Bowie knife, 11, 33, 46, 54, 91
Brown, Owen (father), 6–8, 9

California, 27–30
Calvinism, 6, 8–9, 11
civil rights, 88, 91, 94, 98
Civil War, the, 50, 66, 83–84, 87, 89, 92
Clay, Henry, 27–28
Compromise of 1850, the, 27–30

Declaration of Independence, the, 15–16, 55, 85
disenfranchisement, 94
Douglass, Frederick, 40, **41**, 42, 55, 57–58, 78, 92
Du Bois, W. E. B., 94

Emerson, Ralph Waldo, 79–80, 83
emigrant aid company, 31

fire-eaters, 71
Free Staters, 34, **35**, 43–46, 50, 52, 56
free states, **14**, 20, 22–23, 26, 28–30, 34, 45, 55
fugitives, **18**, 23, 29–30, 33, 38, 41, 53, 58
Fugitive Slave Act, 28–29, 37, **81**

gallows, 22, 65, **66**, 80, 83
Garrison, William Lloyd, 12, **13**, 22, 77, 81–82
Golden Rule, the, 40, 65
Green, Shields, 57–58

Harpers Ferry, 35, 37, 54, 56, 58–61, **58**, 67, 70–71, 73–74, 77–79, 82, 85, 92, 94, 96, 99

Jefferson, Thomas, 16, 19, 72
"John Brown's Body," 83–84

Kansas-Nebraska Act, 30–31
Kennedy Farm, 57, 59, 78

Langston, Charles, 85, **86**, 87
Lee, General Robert E., 61
Lincoln, Abraham, 76–77, 82
Louisiana Purchase, 19–20
Lovejoy, Elijah P., 22–23, **24–25**
lynching, 22, 33, 64, 94

Index

manifest destiny, 19, 26
martyr, 22, 47, 65, 68, 74, 79–81, 83, 88, 94, 98
Mexican-American War, 23, 26–27, 79
Mexican Cession, 27, 30
militia, 38, 44–46, 48, 60, 68
Missouri Compromise, 20, 23, 27, 30–31, **35**
moral suasion, 12

National Association for the Advancement of Colored People (NAACP), 94–95
normal school, 92

Osawatomie, **36**, 42, **43**, 44, 50–53

pike, 54, 59
popular sovereignty, 28, 30–31
Pottawatomie Massacre, 48–51
Pottawatomie Rifles, 46, 48, 50
predestination, 9
prison letters, 63, 66, 68, 70
Protestantism, 8, 11

secession, 70–71
Secret Six, 53, 78, 84
slave-catchers, 23, 38
slave rebellions, 33, 41, 53, 60, 64, 76, 88
slave states, **14**, 20, 23, 26, 33, **35**, 42, 46, 52,
Storer College, 92, **93**, 94–95, **95**

Sumner, Senator Charles, 46–48

Texas, annexation of, 23, 26, 28
Thoreau, Henry David, 79–80
treason, 38, 40, 45, 64, 72–73, 75, 87
Tubman, Harriet, 57
Turner Rebellion, 41, 60, 88–89, **89**

Underground Railroad, 23, 30
United States Constitution, 12, 16–18, 47, 72

War of 1812, 9
Wise, Governor Henry, 73–74, 76

About the Author

Alison Morretta holds a Bachelor of Arts in English and creative writing from Kenyon College in Gambier, Ohio, where she studied literature and American history. She has written many nonfiction titles for middle and high school students on subjects such as American literature, the abolitionist movement, the civil rights era, westward expansion, and Islamophobia. She lives in New York City with her loving husband, Bart, and their rambunctious Corgi, Cassidy.